POSTDIGITAL PERFORMANCES OF CARE

PERFORMANCE AND DIGITAL CULTURES

Performance and Digital Cultures is a trailblazing and ever-expanding series of critical miniatures, designed to offer timely and ongoing interventions in scholarship on the technologization of performance in rapidly accelerating post-internet cultures. The series combines critical investigations from cutting-edge researchers/practitioners, well-established scholars expanding their expertise to include technologically informed approaches and emergent new voices contributing to the field of intermedial, digital and postdigital performance analysis. With opening provocations and/or forward-thinking manifestos offered by key thinkers, this book series gathers together unique insights on a range of topics that are redefining performance practice in a vastly expanded global convergent culture, in a bite-sized format.

POSTDIGITAL PERFORMANCES OF CARE

TECHNOLOGY AND PANDEMIC

Liam Jarvis and Karen Savage

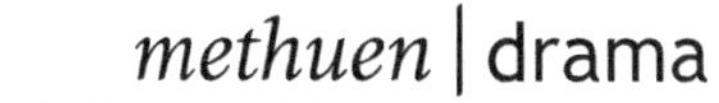

LONDON • NEW YORK • OXFORD • NEW DELHI • SYDNEY

METHUEN DRAMA
Bloomsbury Publishing Plc, 50 Bedford Square, London, WC1B 3DP, UK
Bloomsbury Publishing Inc, 1385 Broadway, New York, NY 10018, USA
Bloomsbury Publishing Ireland, 29 Earlsfort Terrace, Dublin 2, D02 AY28, Ireland

BLOOMSBURY, METHUEN DRAMA and the Methuen Drama logo are trademarks of Bloomsbury Publishing Plc

First published in Great Britain 2024
Paperback edition published 2025

Series design: Ben Anslow
Cover images: Motion Glitch background (© Aleksandra Konoplia / Getty Images); Worker in protective anti-virus clothes cleaning seats in cinema hall with disinfectants. (© Serhii Bobyk / Alamy Stock Photo)

A catalogue record for this book is available from the British Library.

A catalog record for this book is available from the Library of Congress.

ISBN: HB: 978-1-3502-7210-1
PB: 978-1-3502-7211-8
ePDF: 978-1-3502-7213-2
eBook: 978-1-3502-7212-5

Series: Performance and Digital Cultures

Typeset by Newgen KnowledgeWorks Pvt. Ltd., Chennai, India

For product safety related questions contact productsafety@bloomsbury.com.

To find out more about our authors and books visit www.bloomsbury.com and sign up for our newsletters.

CONTENTS

ILLUSTRATIONS

ACKNOWLEDGEMENTS

We would like to thank the University of Essex and the University of Lincoln for supporting this research, and Proto-type Theater for contributing the opening provocation to this book.

SERIES EDITORS' PREFACE

Performance and Digital Cultures is a trailblazing series of short books, designed to offer timely interventions in scholarship on the technologization of performance in rapidly accelerating post-internet cultures. The series collates cutting-edge critical investigations from researchers/practitioners, well-established scholars expanding their expertise to include technologically informed approaches and emergent new voices contributing to the field of intermedial, digital and postdigital performance analysis. With opening provocations offered by key thinkers and makers, this book series gathers unique insights on a range of topics that are redefining expanded performance practices in convergent culture, in a bite-sized format.

Like pressing the 'refresh' button on an internet browser, the series seeks to dislodge fixed and static ideas to explore what has been updated in the analysis of performance with the reloading of the page. With the proliferation of technologies from smartphones to Artificial Intelligence (AI), the ongoing impacts of 'the digital' can be seen everywhere. This series sets out with the ambitious intention to respond to the scale and rapid pace of change. Technological innovation brings about new affordances and shifting ethical considerations, likewise performance forms continue to evolve with the emergent possibilities. As a word around which to gather a book series, 'digital' is a highly prolific but also problematically non-specific concept that carries a range of multifarious uses and possible underlying assumptions, often connected rightly or wrongly to ideas of 'progress' and 'innovation'. And yet the coupling of 'digital' with 'culture' as an umbrella term can become troublingly singular; 'digital culture' runs the danger of untethering technologies, their provenance and effects from specific local impacts, manifestations and individual expression through performance. Michael Connor has similarly argued that what was once articulated as 'internet culture' is increasingly now just 'culture', recognizing a shift from something once discrete to the 'reconfiguration of all culture by the internet, or by internet-enabled neoliberal capitalism' (Connor 2013). The plural word 'cultures' in this series' title seeks to recognize and analyse the global reach of our digital interconnectedness, while recognizing that which is distinct and contingent. From within the hegemonic forces of internet-enabled capitalism, where can outside positions be recuperated to gain critical perspective on developments in performance? This series seeks to create a space for authors to self-reflexively examine the implications of performances that are ever adapting to the kinds of displacements and reconfigurations that digital cultures continue to generate.

OPENING PROVOCATION: SOFT SPACES; HARD EDGES

Proto-type Theater

Some questions, no answers

Karen Savage and Liam Jarvis contacted us about this introduction mid-2022. They said they were writing a book on care, technology and performance and had some questions for us:

> What were our experiences as a small company of theatre-makers and artists during the Covid-19 pandemic? How did we *care for each other*, as friends, colleagues, humans?
> How did the sector *care for itself*?
> *Did* the sector care for itself?
> Was there help?
> How did we care for the work we make together?
> How is it now post-Covid-19 … ?
> … if that's even where we are.

These are questions we've asked ourselves, questions that are now extended, ongoing, conversations we're having as a company – as friends, colleagues, humans.

We're a small company but we like to think we look bigger on the outside (kind of like an inverse-TARDIS). In reality, there are three of us – Rachel, Gillian and Wes – and we've worked together for (about) fifteen years.

We've created a host of multidisciplinary projects over this time, with our core work primarily being devised touring theatre – frequently political, often experimental, always contemporary. When we work on these projects, our company expands, and we work with freelance designers, artists, performers, technicians and composers. We support young and emerging artists, provide paid internships and mentoring, and offer as much participatory activity as we can. We form partnerships with funders, arts venues and theatres across the UK and beyond. We share the work widely, meeting and talking to audiences about art and politics, asking questions about the changes they want to see in the world.

When we work, we expand. We expand in numbers, and in possibility, and in impact. Everything we do is made *with* and *for* people, and to be shared in person, in spaces, together.

So, in March 2020, when 'together' became all-of-a-sudden illegal, we became small, and fragile, and all that work and connection stopped. Our sector stopped still, frozen in shock.

Covid-19 posed its own questions – not least of which was 'am I and everyone I love going to die?', followed swiftly by

When will this stop?
Does this stop?
What can I *do*?

As the news tolled grimly and the 'new normal' took its place, questions about work and the future took over, about personal circumstances, about professional responsibilities:

Is this it?
Has our sector gone for good?
How can we keep people employed?
What are we supposed to *do*?
What are we *expected* to do?
What *should* we do?
Where from now?
How?

There were no easy, ready answers, just fear and uncertainty, and an overwhelming desire for connection. The country might have all been 'in it together', but none of us was *actually* together – we had never been so forcibly separate and isolated. Hard edges.

Some answers, more questions

Like many of you reading this, we found and made ways to connect with the things and the people we loved. We hosted quizzes on Zoom, we made pubs the size of a laptop screen, we checked in with friends we perhaps hadn't seen in forever – just because they were now as close by as the ones we saw all the time. Soft spaces.

Schooling and universities moved into the home, we taught from our tables and sofas, meetings became endless seas of little windows, and we held so many of them – sharing our uncertainties and looking for solutions.

Eventually, we started to see theatre again. Initially most pieces were uploads of things gone before, previously recorded works hastily packaged for a new 'digital' audience, with varying degrees of success. Other shows were reworkings of current live work – ported to an online space. Then, over time, new work was created especially for the realm.

Sharing work in online spaces wasn't new – digital art, digital theatre, multi-modal and digital-hybrid art long predated the pandemic – sharing work online *as the only option* was what was actually new.

There was, we felt, an expected level of expertise – that everyone of course just *knew* how to make work for digital spaces – or immediately how to package and upload. That all of us working in a live medium would have perfectly recorded, high-quality, multi-camera setup recordings of the work with high fidelity sound – that we'd essentially be film-makers; *that we'd prepared for this.*

Where this expectation came from is now not too clear – certainly, we were asked by venues if we had anything – but they were polite enquiries, not pressures. Perhaps it came from social media – from seeing other artists, other companies who did have stuff to share and feeling inadequate – after all, comparison is the thief of joy. Maybe, what *we* eventually put out into the world made others feel the same – maybe we compounded the problem, should have been more careful, maybe we should have *taken more care.*

Perhaps, it was hearing from online audiences about *their* experiences, and the increasing feeling of Zoom-ennui – Netflix was a comfort, but theatre does not have those same values – theatre (for us) has an 'eventness' which is always missing from the pre-recorded.

One piece that stood out in that sea of ported content, perhaps because it had been fully reconsidered, was the evening we listened to love songs together in a Zoom-room full of strangers in Uninvited Guests' *Love Letters from Home*. This was a 'joyful and open-hearted Zoom performance' designed to bring 'people together in a time of physical distance from friends and family'. In the world before, this had been a live show: *Love Letters Straight from Your Heart*, which the company described as an 'event that is somewhere between a wedding reception, a wake and a radio dedication show'. Here, it was remade for Zoom to shift 'between theatre and feeling like a real social event'. We watched the piece 'at' Bristol Old Vic on 3 June 2020; two nights later we could have seen the piece 'in' Mexico City and on 10 June, 'visited' both Wales and Los Angeles in the same day.

In advance, we submitted our song requests and arrived at our booked seats (sofas) for curtain up (the start of the Zoom call). The piece did indeed swing between 'performed theatre' and a 'social event', the soft spaces of conversation and socialization, so missing from every other firmly delineated hard-edged Zoom interaction, wrapping themselves around the scripted pre-planned sections. It was funny, and real, and we shed tears and watched others do so too – we cared for each other's current circumstance and loss, and understood more about those we each loved. Soft spaces, hard edges.

This was possibly an affecting experience not only because we shared and sang expressions of love with each other, but also because we were aware of everyone watching with us – those windows into living rooms and kitchens so familiar yet so foreign, into families gathered to watch, into the individuals – the couples separated but briefly together right now, *for this*. We were, most certainly, an audience – sharing not only the digital space but the temporal space – here, live, and in this moment, watching each other watching. The performers joined us, providing (seemingly) 'off-script' and 'real' moments where they turned the camera on their own families and piles of washing – revealing the backstage mechanisms and structures in the metatheatrical ways that contemporary theatre has proven so very good at. Uninvited Guests cared not only for the rigour of the work but also our experience by remaking the work to bring us meaningfully together.

We thought a lot about the 'soft space around the hard edge' while rethinking a summer school we had been due to host with Mansions of the Future (a three-year cultural participation project and hub based in Lincoln, UK). This week-long event had been due to take place in person, across the city, and welcome artists, theatre-makers and creative practitioners from the Midlands to encounter new approaches to creating work and developing their practice. Rather than cancel – or merely port the event – we thought carefully about how we might care for our artists, participants, guest speakers and all of us on the delivery team. We built soft spaces into the schedule – time to breakfast and lunch together, an open-window 'Zoom Room' – which always had someone there to chat to – recognizing that many people were alone and had not shared a meal or even a proper conversation with anyone for (maybe) months. We shortened the session lengths, relaxed the structured content, sent physical, tactile, objects through the post, built well-being sessions into the schedule, and encouraged conversation, sharing and reality to all creep in.

We were fortunate to be in receipt of funding to deliver this event, not only for those who participated but also so we could honour fees for our freelance delivery team as well as the twelve freelance, professional artists and makers who led guest sessions throughout the week. The precarity of the sector was all too apparent at this point – the figure of 70 per cent of the workforce being freelance and therefore under threat was stark, and we joined colleagues and friends in despairingly un-picking, un-producing and un-making work that had potentially taken years of planning, strategizing and funding to create. Planning and un-planning with every new scrambling word from the often-contradictory No.10 podium.

Organizations appeared; Freelancers Make Theatre Work and the Freelancers in the Dark research project were among them, asking questions, calling for solidarity, asking us to consider how we might build back better. They formed groups, held discussions, proposed radical solutions, all in the name of change. Designer Bethany Wells faced the challenge single-handedly and head-on – selling canvas tote bags with the Caryl Churchill quote 'terrible rage' repeated again and again – merchandise for protest but also raising money for freelance artists to help with unpaid bills, lost work, cancelled gigs.

This desire to rebuild asked more questions of us all as a sector – artists, organizations, funders, punters:

> What is the cost of care – reputationally, financially, practically?
> Who pays?
> Who cares?

And then … the 'post-' appears, the after. Beyond that moment of initial horror, and into a new, sustained one. The threats are over (they tell us), but has anything changed? We moved to a new and insidious low-grade hum that we're supposed to block and ignore, to work over and through and round. Business as usual. Theatre is open.

No questions, wrong answers

For the past eight years, our work has been explicitly political, and in-the-room theatre experiences still (*we* think) have a unique currency in that regard. Our 2015 show, *A Machine They're Secretly Building* (*AMTSB*) quite literally couldn't have been a film, or a piece of digital or transmedial content because of the law. *AMTSB* was about state-sponsored surveillance (particularly, the Edward Snowden revelations), and in it we told our audiences things that would have been subject to a Defence and Security Media Advisory-Notice (or 'D-Notice'), which is a government request (and one which has never not been granted), not to publish or broadcast certain information on the grounds of national security. It was, our government felt, a matter of national security to not let the British public know about the ways in which they were being illegally surveilled.

The theatre then, which wasn't subject to the same scrutiny of film, television or print, was for us a place of political care, about care for the truth. It told us what 'belonged' in those spaces and gave them an edge. Is there a danger, perhaps, that multi-modal or hybrid-digital works might not be afforded those same political freedoms? It seems a silly thing to say, when you think about the early political years of the internet as a mobilizing, enabling force for change. But where online space worked towards a democratization of knowledge, the energy from that explosion has invigorated extremism, multiplied those with extremist positions and pushes out algorithmically curated 'truth' which fragments and destabilizes any attempt at a political discourse of care. Less soft space, more hard edge.

And what of resilience? It is a laudable virtue, to be able to muster some resolve in difficult moments, to get knocked down and get back up again. But doesn't it depend on who's asking for it? Too often resilience is a sugar-coating for being okay with things getting worse, with suffering privations that – in a caring and compassionate society – we ought not have to suffer. Resilience appears too often as a smokescreen for the interests of capital, or to excuse the failings of power.

When resilience becomes a self-starting enterprise, it lets others off the hook for behaving well. In the UK, recent changes to Arts Council England funding guidelines have, through the 'Let's Create' strategy, placed the social (and moral?) responsibility for care and social welfare at the doorstep of a sector of artists neither fully equipped nor trained to fulfil those vital social functions. And, of course, artists will do it – likely unequipped and untrained – but invited in by those in power and holding the purse strings. The competitive nature of public funding in the UK will see too few questions asked about who is actually appropriate to deliver on the impact promise made by the National Portfolio Organisations, and what the long-term implications are of handing over what should be the responsibility of a Department for Health and Social Care to an arms-length branch of the Department for Culture, Media and Sport.

Throughout the pandemic, there was an enormous energy in the sector for change. Meaningful, sweeping, revolutionary change.

Change away from the funding merry-go-round, away from the army of experienced freelance professionals relying on in-and-out contracts that add up to less than minimum wage. There seemed to be an appetite to rebuild it all, until … there wasn't. Audiences started to come back, those familiar things we loved about our industry, that we loved in spite of how broken it was, felt comforting, felt good. With a rusted groan, the big wheels started to turn again, organizations opened their doors and, a relaunch 'party' and season brochure later, went back to the way things were. Hauntingly, the UK arts sector 'post'-Covid-19 added significant weight to Fredric Jameson's sobering prospect that it's easier to imagine an end to the world than an end to capitalism. For a moment we thought we might have been looking at the end of the world, and imagination hardly seemed necessary. And yet even as we sat on the brink, the idea of something different eluded us.

Rachel Baynton, Gillian Lees, Andrew Westerside
Proto-type Theater
Lincoln and Glasgow, December 2022

INTRODUCTION: A 'POSTDIGITAL PANDEMIC'?

The Covid-19 disease, caused by the SARS-CoV-2 virus, has been described as a 'digital pandemic' (Okano-Heijmans 2020) – firstly, in terms of its origin, with researchers such as Makoto Yokozawa arguing that the spread of the virus was exacerbated by the Chinese government's restrictions on the digital dissemination of information (e.g. warnings about early cases of infection); secondly, in terms of its effect with governments around the world 'resorting to digital instruments to combat the virus' (Okano-Heijmans 2020). Unquestionably, a wide variety of digital mitigations were used, from big data analytics to track disease transmission using mobile phone geolocalization (Serafino et al. 2022) to the application of artificial intelligence to accelerate diagnoses (Wang et al. 2021). But a further characteristic of the 'digital pandemic' was the increased reliance of the public on digital channels of communication from within governmentally imposed lockdown restrictions to contain the virus. Covid-19 may not have been the first 'post-internet' pandemic, with the H1N1pdm09 virus circulating globally in 2009, but it was the first to result in quarantines on a vast global scale that drove users online en masse from their domestic spaces to work, learn, stay in touch and access basic services; including the pivot for audiences to access pre-recorded and live-streamed theatrical performances on the internet, which Proto-type discuss in their opening provocation.

Unsurprisingly, according to data collected by the International Telecommunication Union (ITU), uptake of the internet accelerated rapidly during this time. Pre-pandemic in 2019, 4.1 billion people (54 per cent of the world's population) were using the internet. Mid-pandemic, this surged by 782 million to reach 4.9 billion people in 2021 (63 per cent of the population) (ITU 2022). But notably this statistic also points to 37 per cent of the global population who remained offline, for whom access to the affordance of online communication was limited, or non-existent. The reach of the 'digital' while widespread is, at best, uneven. In relation to care, this raises the question of who the framing of the Covid-19 as a 'digital pandemic' leaves behind? Furthermore, what epistemologies of 'theatre' were ruptured when the pandemic accelerated a digital turn that was already in the ascendency, and how were digital communication technologies used caringly or uncaringly at a moment of significant vulnerability?

This project analyses imbrications between artistic and social/healthcare practices mid-pandemic, and the mediation of care through, and *as*, communications technologies. We examine 'performance' in its expanded sense, taking as objects of analyses a diverse array of transmediated theatrical performances, online memes, films, the online optics of political actors/policymakers and performances of the everyday as both displays of, and counter-narratives towards, mid-pandemic resilience. At root, we will be asking '*who* cares?', examining the limits of practices that digitally care for others at a distance within the confines of global quarantines. The original dimension of this research is our synthesizing of different performative phenomena in order to critique the widespread spectacularization of care towards different ends, focusing on the obstructed 'offstage' (offline) areas that have been overlooked in between different digital spaces. This emphasis has enabled us to rethink evolving notions of 'resilience' and how, as artists, we can continue to create work that cares.

The word 'care' can mean different things in different contexts. Michael Fine articulated care as a fundamental attribute for maintaining life and the basis for the development of essential components of social life (Fine 2005). Issues surrounding caring and protecting others pervaded most aspects of life amidst the Covid-19 health crisis, and digital communication played a crucial role in maintaining or recuperating 'social life' when face-to-face contact became limited. The increased reliance on digital technologies as a crutch mid-pandemic, combined with the drive from governments to gather data on their populations like never before, led to widespread concerns about the pandemic normalizing digital instruments of mass surveillance (Eck and Hatz 2020). It is this tension between the emergent possibilities of digital solutions to a global health crisis, and pervasive unease about their potential longer-term applications, which we argue have prompted a reconsideration of the 'digital pandemic' as a '*postdigital* pandemic'. The 'postdigital' is typified in this context by disenchantment with digital information systems, concern for who a 'digital pandemic' might exclude, and the impacts of asymmetrical power structures between corporate big tech media platforms and their users. Just prior to the pandemic, investigative journalist, Carole Cadwalladr, described the ethical task of holding big tech to account as a problem that is 'so big it's like the sun. You can't look at it directly' (Cadwalladr 2019). The notion of the postdigital, we propose, encourages an examination of the blind spots of digital culture mid-pandemic: practices that might not be read as 'digital' on the surface, but represent displacements in the wake of digital activity that require critical attention. From the use of vacant theatre buildings as courtrooms when theatre practices migrated online to the ethical implications of theatre reimagined across various mediums, old and new – what passed as 'theatre' became broad enough to encompass everything from 'Zoom plays' to performances as self-generating experiences sent by post, necessitating an expanded understanding of performance.

Transmediation was widespread mid-pandemic, which Lars Elleström had defined as the transferring of media characteristics from one medium to another (Elleström 2014). When audiences could not convene in shared physical space, theatre practices shifted rapidly to other mediums as a survival reflex. For our purposes, 'postdigital performances' mid-pandemic are less a coherent aesthetic trend or genre; hybridized practices such as 'internet theatre' (Lavender 2017), 'telematic performance' (Chatzichristodoulou 2014), 'cyberperformance' or 'cyberstages' (Papagiannouli 2011) and 'networked performance' (Pérez 2014) were all nothing new. Aesthetic movements were subordinate to necessity in relation to the shock of a public health scare. As Proto-type highlighted, the pandemic prompted many makers working in live mediums to feel they should immediately possess an 'expected level of [digital] expertise'; that they should somehow *already* know how to counter the sudden barriers that global lockdowns had posed to reaching isolated audiences. Furthermore, the loss of shared 'in-the-room' experiences with the closure of theatre buildings raised political issues about 'the digital' and what *could* be performed or said online. This is evident in Prototype's revealing example of their show, *A Machine They're Secretly Building*, which, as non-networked and off-grid 'theatre', escaped being subject to a DSMA-Notice to prevent wider digital circulation of the information shared on national security grounds. Ironically, theatre's forced lean into the digital realm online mid-pandemic also represented a lean into further restrictions as to what can be shared with audiences in some cases, even in countries with significant internet freedoms.

As ubiquitous as the 'digital' solutions, prompted by the mass upheaval of the pandemic, were the ethical sensitivities about how to 'care' for one another in a radically altered landscape. And how to deliver performances that rejuvenated social life caringly. The pandemic brought into sharp relief that 'care' is not something *different* from technology and its applications (an idea examined in relation to 'digital care' in Chapter 4). And yet care was something that could easily be reduced to mere spectacle for political expediency through the circulation of information online (discussed in Chapter 3). A central thread of this book is an examination and deconstruction of 'spectacles of resilience' that we argue apprehended imagery associated with care mid-pandemic to responsibilize individuals, while often acting as a smokescreen to the ongoing neglect of systems of care and the material conditions of caregivers working within them; with theatre-makers sometimes filling in as stopgap social service providers (Chapter 1). Throughout the book, we work towards the notion of 'meta-resilience' – 'meta' deriving from the Greek *μετά* ('beyond') – to consider the kinds of resiliencies that might be necessitated by the 'embodied internet' of the metaverse, for both its users and for performance-makers online. More widely, we use the term 'meta-resilience' as a kind of thought experiment; a speculative concept to contemplate future resilience in consideration of the new normalcies that may arrive post-pandemic (Chapter 5).

The emphasis on care has often been as an interpersonal dynamic, which is epitomized by care theorist Nel Noddings's notion of direct 'caring for' others (discussed in Chapter 4). But the restrictions and heightened risk level involved in meeting the faces of others mid-pandemic made the navigation of face-to-face contact inextricable from notions of care. This is possibly why the pandemic rejuvenated critical interest in the caring implications of Jewish philosopher Emmanuel Levinas's ethical notion of the radical alterity bound up in the face-to-face encounter (Levinas 1969). The coalescing of Levinasian face ethics with the absence of face-to-face encounters in quarantine hinted alarmingly at the possibility of an oncoming ethical crisis in addition to a public health crisis (which we examine in Chapter 2). Notably, Levinasian ethics emerged from a historically specific moment following the Nazi genocide of European Jews during the Second World War, in which the attempt to eliminate an entire people was orchestrated through processes of rational organization. Levinas shifted Martin Heidegger's philosophical emphasis from a pursuit of 'being' the most authentic realization of who you are to instead emphasizing one's responsibility for the 'Other'. But in wresting face ethics from its historical moment to a post-internet culture that Levinas couldn't have foreseen, how might his ideas be rethought amidst the global postdigital pandemic? And *can* they be? Especially when the very face-to-face encounters that are central to moral valence in Levinasian thought posed a known public health risk since the first reported cases of Covid-19 in late December 2019 in Wuhan (World Health Organisation 2020). The World Health Organization's director-general Tedros Ghebreyesus's claim mid-pandemic that 'no-one is safe until everyone is safe', foregrounded an ethics akin to Levinas's, bound-up in one's personal responsibility towards the protection of vulnerable others. Given these resonances, we will consider how Levinasian 'ethical encounters' – which Nicholas Ridout proposed that theatre was an apt space to host on account of its potential to reconnect 'perception and experience' (Ridout 2009: 58) – were impacted by the transmediation of theatre online mid-lockdown. A force majeure like the Covid-19 pandemic is, by its very nature, an almost unimaginably expansive global phenomenon.

Like Cadwalladr's metaphor for holding big tech to account, to gaze at the pandemic's effects is like staring into the sun. We recognize that there is a politics around what gets included in this critical discussion and what does not; a sensitivity that is further exacerbated within the limits of a short volume. While we try to capture an international outlook on postdigital performance, care and technology, we start from our own geographical restrictions and points of reference in our selection of practices and cultural phenomena to analyse. This book was co-authored, in part, from within our own respective lockdowns; with Karen Savage subject to strict *quedarse en casa* ('stay at home') restrictions while on a short vacation in Andalusia that became a ten-week quarantine, and then later the tiered restrictions in the UK. Liam Jarvis was in lockdown exclusively in the UK, teaching Drama students at the University of Essex from his family's home on the Isle of Wight when the prospect of travel became impossible. Our UK-focus is interspersed with examples of a diverse array of global arts practices that circulated online. We draw out resonances between healthcare professionals and artists, focusing on the ways that technology was used to facilitate artistic encounters, as well as medical ones. We bridge these areas by exploring the ways that healthcare workers used arts practices to care for themselves and their communities, and we examine the way that care was spectacularized by political actors.

1
SPECTACLES OF RESILIENCE: POSTDIGITAL TENSIONS

In September 2020, global quarantines intended to suppress the spread of the Covid-19 virus closed theatre buildings around the world. Digital platforms became proxy stages, hosting not only the live arts that migrated from public buildings, but also more pervasive performances of the everyday. Screen media became a space through which to both perform and undercut notions of individual resilience by making visible the hidden realities of our domestic spaces. One example was Environmental Engineer Gretchen Goldman, who was interviewed remotely from her home by CNN for a news segment in which she expressed her concerns about former US president Donald Trump's appointment of a climate change denier in a top governmental agency position.[1] Afterwards, Goldman shared a humorous tweet that went viral online containing two images; a screenshot from her CNN interview and an off-camera photo of her home (see Figure 1.1). In the latter, we see her chaotic domestic environment, with a laptop stacked up on a dining room chair that's balanced precariously on top of a coffee table. She's surrounded by children's toys shuffled out of the judgemental gaze of her webcam.

During global lockdown restrictions, internet users were widely trained to perform for surveillance technologies. Various websites offered practical guidance on home-working and looking professional online 'from the waist up' (Skeete-Cross 2020). YouTube tutorials provided tips on how users could hide their domestic environments for work-related video calls using background-concealing filters such as Zoom's 'virtual backgrounds' function. But what Goldman's tweet intentionally unconceals through her social media channels is

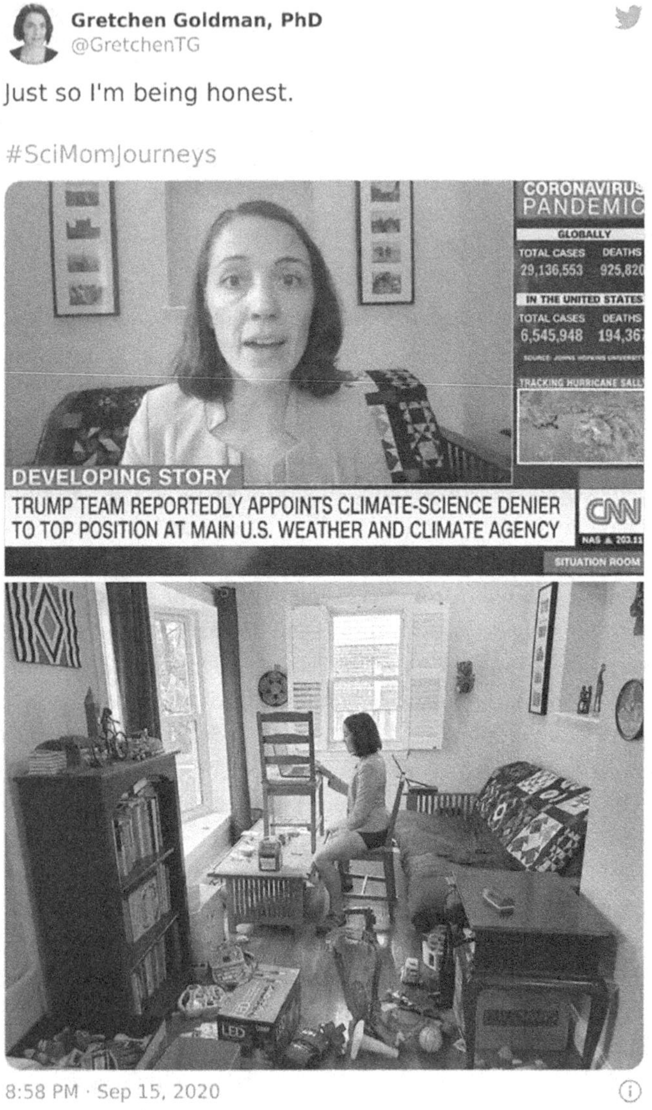

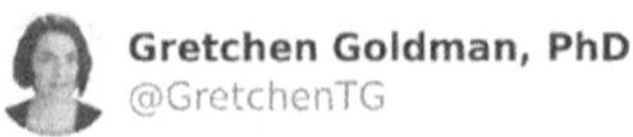

Just so I'm being honest.

#SciMomJourneys

8:58 PM · Sep 15, 2020

Figure 1.1 Tweet by Gretchen Goldman (@GretchenTG, 15 September 2020) © Gretchen Goldman, 2020.

the messy remnants of her otherwise invisible care labour. This is a personal disclosure that brings signifiers of care back into the frame at a time when governments around the world, to varying degrees, failed to protect social care, care workers and care home residents from the seismic impacts of Covid-19. A startling example of this was a landmark ruling by the High Court in 2022, which determined that the UK government's policy to discharge people from hospitals to care homes in the first weeks of the pandemic without testing was 'illegal' (Booth 2022).

Goldman's photo is a useful exemplar of everyday performances that indexically reference the material labour involved in balancing childcare responsibilities with a professional media appearance from within a domestic setting. That Goldman is 'appropriately' dressed *only* from the 'waist up', while sitting in her shorts/underpants, acts as a reminder that with the widespread conflation of our private/public spheres mid-pandemic, caring responsibilities and other aspects of professional life had, for many, become increasingly difficult to disentangle. In lockdown conditions, internet users were only ever a mis-judged camera-angle away from bringing signifiers of their domestic caring duties into the picture. By deliberately sharing phenomena lurking 'offstage' that are obscured by other media – a phenomenon mid-pandemic that we refer to as '*off-staging*' throughout this book – Goldman poses a challenge to what we describe as 'spectacles of resilience'. This term combines 'spectacle' in Guy Debord's sense of mediating representations of consumer capitalism that pacify or distract with the word 'resilience', deriving in part from the post-classical Latin word *resilientia*, or the 'fact of avoiding' ('resilience'). Spectacles of resilience are a cultural 'filter' of a kind, staging and circulating signifiers of care online, but often as a smokescreen to inaction in policymaking or the uncaring/neglectful systems from which they divert attention. By contrast, Goldman's tweet emphasizes her labour as a mother, which simply cannot be recognized through her CNN performance. This performance of the everyday coincides with other kinds of theatrical labour that economic recovery measures similarly rendered invisible during the pandemic, such as freelance theatre professionals in the gig economy who could not work, were not eligible for governmentally supported furlough schemes and whose pre-pandemic contributions went unrecognized or undervalued.

Online theatre and mid-pandemic resilience

'Resilience', depending on its usage, can be a particularly complex and problematic term. In relation to defence-speak on 'national resilience', Kenneth Weisbrode and Heather H. Yeung have noted that there is 'no perfect state of resilience' and that the more people seek resilience 'the more each individual will look to their surroundings (which includes other individuals) as a threat'. This means they are 'more likely to turn to ever more blatant and expensive performances of "resilience", instead of attempting to achieve a resilient state' (Weisbrode and Yeung 2020). Weisbrode and Young critique government and media-driven 'resilience theatre', where the language/performance of resilience is detached from resilience itself and becomes antithetical to its stated aim; to make us safer and more resilient. The concept of 'resilience' has long been a topic of analysis across a range of disciplinary fields. In psychology, within the study of child development since the 1970s, the notion of the 'resilient child' became synonymous with individuals who had 'special' character traits (Rutter 1987, cited in Young, Green and Rogers 2008: 41). Resilience of this kind was considered out of the ordinary. Later, 'ecological' approaches to understanding resilience shifted the focus from individuals to relationships *between* individuals and their environments (Ungar 2004). But this approach assumed that resilience was underpinned by 'normative development', which scholars in disability studies have long argued can be damaging by excluding disabled people from the category of 'resilient' (Runswick-Cole and Goodley 2013). This draws attention to problems around how 'resilience' is defined – especially when it is conceptualized only in terms of individual characteristics – since exclusion from resilience as a category can lead to individuals being blamed for their 'perceived lack of inner strength to overcome "their lot in life"' (Ungar 2005: 91). The pervasive global impacts of the pandemic have further emphasized our interdependency to the extent that 'resilience' thought of as an individualistic trait makes little sense. Our resilience is inextricably connected both to others as well as the technologies we can access/leverage, which is why the global drive towards equitable vaccine distribution was 'a humanitarian imperative' (UNICEF 2021); 'no-one is safe until *everyone* is safe'.

Of more relevance to our interdependencies mid-pandemic, in the study of socio-ecological systems, the notion of 'resilience' against the backdrop of the Anthropocene has been applied to reconnect human activity to the biosphere. This re-emphasizes the interconnectedness of, and dependencies between, nature and human society. In this context, 'resilience thinking' has described how interacting systems of people and nature can be managed in the face of disturbances, surprises and uncertainty (Walker and Salt 2006). But for our purposes in this book, mid-pandemic 'spectacles of resilience' promote adapting to and recovering from adversity expedited by the Covid-19 virus, while placing an emphasis squarely on individual responsibility, often to 'avoid' or deflect blame for systemic failures. Spectacles of resilience tend to draw attention to our social reality as a non-stop stream of images of gratitude and solidarity online. Such images accord with Debord's notion of spectacle as instruments society uses to unify itself, while simultaneously maintaining separation. Frequently, images have even separated the one/s caring from the one/s cared for in acts of 'digital care' (discussed further in Chapter 4). The pandemic has sent Debord's 1967 thesis – that all facets of people's lives are mediated by spectacles – into hyperdrive, especially when the circulation of representations competing for our attention online became substitutionary to direct face-to-face contact in various aspects of our lives.

While still mid-pandemic at the time of writing across 2021/22/23 – when the full extent of the pandemic on the theatre industry remains difficult to fully predict in the long term – early indicators suggest a variety of detrimental impacts, many of which are linked to the increasing complexity of having to be independently 'resilient' and juggling freelance work with caring responsibilities. For example, the *Women in Theatre Survey* (Tuckett 2021) led by Research and Literary Director of Sphinx Theatre company, Jennifer Tuckett, investigated the impacts of the coronavirus pandemic on women specifically. It revealed that many were concerned about structural imbalances where caring challenges had fallen disproportionately to women. Lack of financial support for freelance parents and those with caring responsibilities meant that out of the 387 respondents, 61 per cent of women across all roles in UK theatre reported that they were considering leaving the industry (Tuckett 2021: 18), while 85 per cent were worried that gender inequality would worsen post-pandemic (Tuckett 2021: 14). Two years later, *The Big Freelancer Survey 2023* report from Freelancers Making Theatre Work in the UK provided further justification for these concerns, identifying a gender pay gap of 37.4 per cent among the 1,126 freelancer respondents in the industry who contributed. The lack of support for freelance women balancing increased caring challenges amidst the crisis is compounded by wider perceptions of a lack of care at a governmental level towards the arts and culture sectors more broadly, with the Conservative party's chief strategist at the time, Dominic Cummings, alleged to have said in a Zoom meeting about pandemic support for the arts that 'the fucking ballerinas can get to the back of the queue' (Masterson 2020). This signals a profound problem mid-pandemic of conceiving of 'resilience' as an 'individual' characteristic when the range of impacts have been unequal[2] and the distribution of economic support for different sectors has similarly been weighted inequitably, further disadvantaging those with caring duties. For example, many precarious freelance theatre workers could not access the Self-Employment Income Support Scheme (SEISS) in the UK, such as those who took on a mixture of PAYE employment and freelance work, those who hadn't been freelancing for long enough to qualify and self-employed people whose profits were too low. The latter group includes those who experienced gaps in their earnings due to parental leave or other kinds of caring responsibilities (Saville 2020). This is just one respect in which the care labour of freelance workers in the theatre industry was not valued through the UK government's economic support packages.

In 2021, the UK government published a 'Call for Evidence', encouraging the public to contribute to the vision for a 'National Resilience Strategy'. The purpose of this consultation was to prepare for future challenges and develop a resilient society with 'flexible response structures that can adapt and respond to the unexpected' (Cabinet Office 2021: 7). Notably, the definition of 'resilience' offered by the Cabinet Office in this document was synonymous with 'bouncing back'; the ability to 'quickly recover from a difficult situation' (12). But bouncing 'back' could be interpreted to imply a recovery to a 'usual' state, or a desirable return to a pre-pandemic 'normal'. In contrast, playwright Caridad Svich argued on Twitter – rebranded in 2023 by Elon Musk as 'X' – that there is no 'reset' to a 2019 normality. For Svich, we are 'interpandemic' and the current cultural moment marked by accelerated change invites theatre-makers to 'embrace audio, digital, streaming and hybrid' in order to imagine a 'more accessible, inventive, equitable field' (Svich 2021).[3] Svich's call for visioning a future of blended and hybridized modes of theatre practice might be connected to earlier concepts such as Mark Robinson's notion of organizational 'adaptive resilience' in the arts post-economic crisis, which concerned 'adapting with integrity in response to changing circumstances' (Robinson 2010). Resilience of this kind concerns arts organizations cultivating 'adaptive skills' (innovation embedded in reflective practice) and applying them with 'clearly defined vision and purpose' (Robinson 2010: 29).

Chinese theatre director Wang Chong's 'Online Theater Manifesto' arguably went further than Svich by claiming that the pandemic has brought into sharp relief the fact that unlike restaurants, factories and Netflix, theatre 'became non-essential long ago' (Chong 2020). Chong describes online theatre as 'a prelude to our future' in a manifesto that concludes with a rallying call to artists to 'stand still, or join us' (Chong 2020). But this injunction is paradoxical; at once liberatory and potentially passive to the hegemonic forces driving technological evolution and silent on the political forces that would seek to curb such online freedoms. For example, Chong's techno-utopian argument that online spaces offer a public 'forum' long since absent from theatre buildings, where artists can 'control all language and symbols', is perhaps overly optimistic when according to Freedom House's 'Freedom on the Net 2021' report, China ranked as the worst environment for internet freedom for the seventh year in a row.

Furthermore, the Covid-19 pandemic was among the 'most heavily censored topics' online in China (Shahbaz and Funk 2021). The convergences of media formats and possibilities of 'internet theatre' as part of a resilience strategy are highly contingent when there are diverging levels of state intervention in regulating the internet, with some artists operating in global territories with significant internet freedom and others working in a political climate of digital authoritarianism.

A postdigital attitude: The glitching of digital culture

Returning to the example of Gretchen Goldman's tweet, the deconstruction of spectacles of resilience online and foregrounding of disorderly domestic lockdown environments has correspondence with a 'postdigital' sensibility in aesthetics, which pulls focus on that which is obstructed in digital culture by emphasizing glitches and the messiness that lurks beneath the veil of shiny interfaces. While Goldman does not seek to foreground the computational processes underlying her tweet in the way a 'glitch artist' might, she draws attention to the glitching effect that the pandemic has had on culture more broadly; the pandemic-*as*-glitch. Beyond technical malfunction, the word 'glitch' can also mean a 'sudden short-lived irregularity in behaviour' ('Glitch'). While the far-reaching impacts of the pandemic may be far from 'short-lived', one irregularity amidst lockdown conditions has been the necessity for domestic spaces to 'act' as mis-cast classrooms, offices, theatre stages, and so on. Resilience of a more superficial kind – synonymous with the 'fact of avoiding' – could look like hiding or minimizing the jarring effects prompted by these kinds of circumspect conflations, for example, Zoom *as* 'theatre' or theatres-*as*-courtrooms. But we propose to scrutinize these convergences. We take a particular interest in the glitching of passive resilience spectacles in digital culture. Goldman's tweet is just one illustration of a prompt to collectively question emergent interpandemic normalities, raising fundamental issues around care that are easily erased through other media. For example, the extent to which blended work/home spaces might potentially jeopardize the very idea of 'home' as a safe space (Canning and Robinson 2021). This interest aligns with wider adjacent projects that have sought to examine inequities produced by digital culture such as 'data feminism', which Catherine D'Ignazio and Lauren F. Klein have argued seeks to draw attention to, and challenge, unequal distributions of power in a data-driven world (D'Ignazio and Klein 2020).

'Postdigital' is a word that has come to mean a variety of different things since the term was coined by American Composer Kim Cascone in 2000. In its attitudinal sense, the word 'postdigital' in the study of aesthetics has been defined by a growing 'disenchantment with digital information systems' (Cramer 2015: 13). A 'postdigital attitude', as we have examined elsewhere (Jarvis and Savage 2021), has steadily emerged from within a hegemonic digital culture typified at its worst by the growing spread of mis/disinformation online, post-truth politics and scepticism towards the dataveillance of internet users by big tech companies and corporate monopolies such as Apple, Amazon, Facebook (now Meta) and Google. This growing disenchantment synonymous with a 'postdigital attitude' has been bolstered by ongoing leaks, disclosures and 'insider' revelations from whistle-blowers from within the tech giant corporations. For example, in 2021 former Facebook data scientist Frances Haugen filed complaints with federal law enforcement in the US following the dissolving of the company's Civic Integrity team. She claimed that the hateful and polarizing content she witnessed on Facebook 'erodes our civic trust' and 'our ability to want to care for each other' (Haugen 2021). Online platforms offering a social lifeline in quarantine have also been called out at a systemic level as unwilling moral arbiters, assisting the spread of hateful content.

Anne Marie Mol proposes that technology is not 'transparent and predictable, but has to be handled with care' (Mol 2008: 5). In terms of design, maintenance and usage, we propose that 'care' is not something *other* than technology. Over-reliance on technologized solutions to the restrictions of movement in global lockdowns elevated platforms such as Zoom to household names, while bringing ethical concerns about whose interests these products were serving to the fore. Critical scrutiny is needed where issues of interpersonal care intersect with the use of social media and personal surveillance technologies as caring mediums – platforms from which caring acts might be performed. What it meant to care, or to '*want* to care', for quarantined others mid-lockdown through the prism of different mediating platforms online was thrown into sharp relief in the absence of direct physical contact. And what caring for online or socially distanced audiences might mean in the way hybridized theatre practices have evolved is ripe for critical exploration. As a global health crisis, the pandemic foregrounded vastly divergent issues of care, from measures to protect oneself and others through access to vaccines and Personal Protective Equipment (PPE), to addressing social and ethnic inequalities manifesting from Covid-19, such as disproportionate risks of infection, mortality rates and increased exposure to loss of income (Platt and Warwick 2020).

We propose that the mass migration of theatrical performances to the internet mid-pandemic necessitates a critical focus on both online practices *and* the physical stage spaces that have been evacuated. This focus aligns with other commentators that have long abandoned digital dualist assumptions that the on and offline are 'separate' when they are enmeshed as an augmented reality where the offline can be increasingly virtual and the online can have everything to do with the 'real world' (Jurgenson 2011). We begin by examining empty theatre buildings and the ethics of care surrounding their alternate usage. A particular focus will be on the controversial temporary use of disused theatre auditoriums such as Salford's The Lowry Theatre as 'Nightingale Courts', a term in the UK that derives from the establishment of temporary hospitals to house the surplus patients created by the Covid-19 pandemic. We will also focus on theatre company Slung Low's Holbeck Club, which became a food bank serving its local community amidst the global crisis, when theatre companies were fulfilling roles more commonly associated with other kinds of social services. While neither represents digital practices per se, the reappropriation of theatre auditoriums for courtroom proceedings was enabled by the displacement of theatre practices to digital spaces. As a kind of real-world augmented reality that superimposed a wholly different societal purpose onto a theatre building, we examine the ethical frictions in the layering of theatre and courtroom. Meanwhile, the transformation of theatre companies to social service providers exposes systemic flaws in social care and enables our postdigital analysis to access theatre-makers engaging communities of elders that a 'digital pandemic' might leave behind.

Vacant theatres as Nightingale Courtrooms

The word 'Nightingale' in 'Nightingale Court' is a reference to nursing pioneer Florence Nightingale, who identified synergies between nursing as a caring profession and the arts by describing it as 'the finest of Fine Arts' (Nightingale 1946). This raises a reciprocal question as to how the arts might care for others in a health crisis? But the reappropriation of arts spaces mid-pandemic towards alternative societal roles introduced complex ethical questions as to how these vacated buildings might provide care. For example, how comfortably do theatre spaces, punitive spaces and the notion of care summoned by the very name 'Nightingale' coalesce when applied to theatres acting as temporary courtrooms? And did the visibility of theatre practices that migrated online create a smokescreen to the uses of less visible and inaccessible theatre buildings mid-crisis?

Salford's The Lowry Theatre was adapted to a Nightingale Court on 25 September 2020, along with hotels the York Hilton and Middlesbrough's Jury Inn. The contract for use lasted about a year, ending on 27 August 2021 (HM Courts & Tribunals Service 2020). The Birmingham Repertory Theatre was also used as a Nightingale Court from December 2020 until July 2021, causing Black British theatre company Talawa to pull out of staging their *Black Joy* season at the theatre; an ambitious body of new work by Black creatives and artists. On 22 December 2020, Talawa tweeted 'earlier this year we announced that the *Black Joy* season would take place at Birmingham Rep in Autumn 2021. Regrettably, this will no longer be the case' (Talawa 2020a). A statement goes on to say, 'The decision Birmingham Rep have taken to host a Nightingale Court does not align with Talawa's commitment to Black artists and communities, the communities most affected by this decision. It has threatened the integrity of the *Black Joy* season; regrettably the partnership is no longer tenable under current circumstances' (Talawa 2020b). The decision to protect the financial sustainability of the theatre by becoming a Nightingale Court could be considered as a caring act on the one hand by keeping the venue running and protecting jobs. However, as Talawa Theatre Company express, the decision affects other communities, those already considered to be vulnerable to the judicial system. The double sadness for these communities was that a safe and creative space became replaced by a courtroom, which is often considered an 'unsafe' space for Black people. And the loss of a season of work particularly created for Black audiences means that these communities potentially feel double the impact. The *Equal Treatment Bench Book* (ETBB) states that 'People from certain minority groups are more likely to be subject to stop and search, arrest and imprisonment, and Black people have very much higher rates of arrest' (Judicial College 2021). Emma Rogerson opined for ayoungertheatre.com on the change of use at The Lowry, saying that '"safety" is an important concept here – to practise the justice system in the same room compromises the inherent safety that theatre should provide. It blasts the door open for the trauma, injustices and deeply private pain which is inseparable from the victims of our justice system' (Rogerson 2020).[4]

One of the most high-profile court cases heard at The Lowry Theatre offers a particularly useful illustrator of the limits of a theatre building's capacity to provide a 'safe' space when its role is changed. This case was against two retired police officers and a solicitor accused of perverting the course of justice in relation to the Hillsborough football disaster. The disaster in 1989 resulted in the death of ninety-six Liverpool football fans after they were crushed in the stadium. The judge ruled that 'there was no case fit for consideration by the jury based on any of the six counts on the indictment' (Lanceley 2021). The impacts have been far-reaching, with a ninety-seventh victim confirmed to have died in 2021, thirty-two years later, as a direct result of injuries sustained at the disaster over three decades prior (Conn and Vinter 2021). A quick Google search will bring up several books written about the disaster, some about the victims and testimonies from people who were there on the day, others about the ongoing injustices. *Beyond Hillsborough* (2014) is a verbatim play by Joanne Halliday and Leyla Dowie, researched in 2011 and 2012. The play includes Hillsborough survivors, journalists, police officers and those who lost family members in the disaster. Anne Williams is one of the voices in the play. Her son Kevin died in the incident, and she set up a registered charity, 'Hope for Hillsborough', to raise funds for legal fees so that the families of victims could seek justice. The play clearly articulates the challenges that the families faced from the police and justice system. Jenni Hicks lost her daughters Sarah and Vicky in the disaster. She says:

> JENNI: the police, the press … I think that's the major thing that's got to come out from this release of documents, that there was a conspiracy … I just hope that there's evidence to back that up … cos you couldn't just get a few coppers fiddling the books and it being this watertight. And the knock-on effect because he hasn't told the truth and the effect it's had on the families' lives … because the truth wasn't told … and it's left us still twenty-three years down the line still looking for truth. (Hicks in Halliday and Dowie 2014: 29)

The theatre (albeit, not specifically The Lowry) had been used to voice the ordeal of survivors and victims. In plays such as *Beyond Hillsborough* a space was created for them to speak their truths about events that day, and their experiences that followed for decades afterwards. The fact that the case fell apart is a sickening injustice for the families of the victims. However, using The Lowry Theatre as a Nightingale Court to hear cases about possible corruption from police and law enforcement implicates theatre spaces in a cruel continuation of the lack of care related to the Hillsborough disaster. The actual presentation of this hearing in a theatre auditorium provides an interesting dynamic to Iain Mackenzie and Robert Porter's methodological approach of 'dramatization' (a well-established concept of Gilles Deleuze (1967)) linking drama and political theory. They argue that 'dramatization is a method aimed at determining the quality of political concepts by "bringing them to life", in the way that dramatic performances bring to life the characters and themes of a playscript' (MacKenzie and Porter 2011: 482). Whereas the reflexive nature of presenting the collapsing tribunal hearing in a theatre building that is unable to act as a theatre, instead performing as a courtroom, creates an ironic and dizzying reiterative performance between the political, legal and arts sectors. This not only revealed a lack of care that had been ongoing throughout the Hillsborough disaster investigations, but also emphasized the wider neglect of arts venues, posing a challenge to the aspirational idea that they might perform as 'safe spaces'.

Theatre as social services: Slung Low and Holbeck Food Bank

Beyond theatres-as-courtrooms, theatre companies had responded to crisis mid-pandemic by acting as social services, when those services were stretched and under intolerable strain. *The Club on the Edge of Town* (2022) is a 'pandemic memoir' written by Alan Lane, who is artistic director of Slung Low Theatre Company. On 7 January 2019, the company took over managing the oldest working men's club in Britain in Holbeck, Leeds. In March 2020, with the club closed due to the pandemic, the company were evaluating how they could continue to be useful to their local community. They wrote a letter to their 200 neighbours, stating that 'the Slung Low team are still here in the office at the club and we are currently healthy and full of energy. We have cars and a van. And you are our neighbours and if there is anything we can do for you in the coming weeks please do not hesitate to ask' (Lane 2022: 69). This invitation resulted in the theatre company undertaking tasks for individual neighbours, and subsequently as part of other charitable organizations. Slung Low worked with Holbeck Food Bank responding to social care referrals, providing more flexibility within the service to support people more regularly with food during the pandemic. This collaboration continued until the end of 2020.

In a candid account of his time spent during the first weeks of lockdown, Lane explains how he responded to an 'invitation to care' when the local City Council called him to take on the social care referrals for the ward, Holbeck and Beeston. With an initial payment of £5,000 from the City Council, Slung Low responded to a range of requests including picking up prescriptions for those shielding, supplying food and helping people with their bin collections. Lane describes a particularly sad and alarming story of a mentally ill woman who thought someone, or something was breaking into her property. Through his efforts to help, Lane reflects on how broken the system is for supporting vulnerable people like this, especially in the context of a pandemic that saw health professionals needing to focus their attention on handling Covid-19 cases. There simply wasn't the time, energy or resource to assist. Additionally, the council had set up restrictions on the amount of food parcels that individuals could receive. If they called the council helpline, they could only be referred for help a total of four times. Slung Low stepped in and encouraged all those using the helpline to call them directly, sending 15,202 parcels out across the duration of the pandemic. The theatre company received multiple calls, not only requests for food and support, but also complaints from disgruntled users of the Holbeck club who felt they were losing a vital 'lifeline'. This spilled over into angry calls:

> On Monday morning there would be a series of voicemails left at the club in a couple of different, elderly but angry northern voices. 'You cheats! We knew you'd betray us as soon as you could. It's disgusting that you've shut our club. DISGUSTING!' And on they went. I don't think these members understood how digital phones work or the joy of 1471. (Lane 2022: 67)[5]

These calls may not have been welcomed by Slung Low, but in terms of communication, the telephone became an emergency flare so that individuals could receive support without being judged or refused, or, in some cases, to vent their frustrations at the situation. Notably, some elderly callers engaged by phone with less barriers than the internet, while not fully understanding the digital telephone technologies with which they were interacting (or that their calls weren't anonymous). Although the theatre company based at the oldest working men's club in Britain had temporarily been forced to close, it could operate as a non-means-tested, self-referral food bank (Lane 2022: 95). The fact that the theatre company was needed to act as a social referral service resonates with Proto-type's opening provocation, with UK arts funding initiatives increasingly placing 'the social (and moral?) responsibility for care and social welfare at the doorstep of a sector of artists neither fully equipped nor trained to fulfil those vital social functions'. When asked 'why does a theatre company run a foodbank?', Lane explains, if he was to put on a show in the carpark of the club within earshot of local residents who were not able to feed their children, then 'that show becomes an act of aggression. A taunting, noisy disturbance' (2022 193). An ailing care system struggling to support people through the pandemic was being bolstered by industrious, if ill-equipped arts organizations, highlighting how long-term care and adequate infrastructure for communities had long been neglected. But this substitutionary patching over of the cracks in the care system was a far cry from Florence Nightingale's historic assertion that caring vocations such as nursing should be the 'finest of Fine Arts'.

Having surveyed different understandings of 'resilience' and its spectacularization online mid-pandemic, and having scrutinized what was taking place in less visible evacuated theatre buildings offline, we now consider an ethical problem through the lens of Emmanuel Levinas's face ethics. Namely, the absence of direct face-to-face encounters in theatre practices that are predicated on presence in shared space and contact with the faces of others.

2
THEATRE'S 'LOSS OF FACE': THE LEVINASIAN PROBLEM OF FACE-TO-FACE ENCOUNTERS MID-PANDEMIC

Theatre during the Covid-19 pandemic experienced a 'loss of face'.[1] This is an apt idiom both in the sense of losing the direct face-to-face encounters on which not only the practice of theatre (excluding hybrid formats such as live broadcast theatre etc.) and Levinasian ethics are predicated, but also, in the sense of being subjected to humiliation; 'to lose face'. Mid-pandemic we witnessed a theatre that was, quite literally, unable to show its face in many instances through performing bodies in shared physical space. For Levinas, the face – which encompasses the other's *weakness* and *vulnerability* – imposes upon us by creating responsibility that is rooted in shame. What is shameful is the feeling 'that we cannot hide what we should like to hide' of ourselves from the other (Levinas 2003: 64). Gretchen Goldman's tweet, as an act of off-staging discussed in Chapter 1, illustrated just how easily representations through media can filter out vulnerabilities associated with care labour. As Claudia Welz explains, in shame 'we are directly confronted with ourselves as connected to others, and therefore, we cannot flee into irresponsibility' (Welz 2011). Levinas's 'Other' is an unknowable, irreducible alterity that cannot be contained, fully comprehended or possessed in thought. It is the exteriority of the face that ensures the other's unique separateness as an entity irreducible to an 'I'. And it is the face that confers upon us an 'infinite' responsibility for another person. Crucially, the absenting of direct face-to-face encounters while quarantined, through a Levinasian lens, has moral implications because it hides the naked vulnerability of the face and potentially diminishes our felt responsibility towards the other. It's important to note that social theorists such as Nick Couldry and Andreas Hepp have problematized binary distinctions between 'pure' face-to-face communications and media, arguing that our 'face-to-face interaction is continuously interwoven with media-related practices' (Couldry and Hepp 2016: 17). However, lockdowns skewed the construction of our social world in many cases to privilege communication 'through' screen media, a fact that is epitomized by the characterization of a 'digital pandemic'.

'Humiliation' is defined in the *Oxford English Dictionary* as 'abasement' in the sense of devaluing and theatre's 'loss of face' marked humiliation for the discipline in myriad ways. Firstly, the vulnerability that theatrical labour entailed through the hazardous act of meeting the face of audiences mid-pandemic meant that the practice posed a higher health risk than other cultural activities. Secondly, the pandemic exposed economic vulnerabilities and the 'fragile economic model' underlying most live theatre events (Davenport 2020). As a result, the shutdown of theatre buildings globally posed catastrophic financial consequences (Brownlee 2021). The decrease in audience capacity with the imposing of social distancing restrictions became unsustainable for some arts venues, with the UK government's Culture Recovery Fund distributing a £1.57 billion support package to provide financial help. However, the impossible challenge for many freelancers to be independently resilient (the understanding of resilience that we critiqued in Chapter 1), in turn, allowed the practice to fall victim to uncaring governmental policies that were selective in who received support. In terms of economic support packages, 'resilience' mid-pandemic equated to the 'fact of avoiding' the needs of gig economy freelancers. In the UK alone, over half of theatre freelancers in an interim report by Freelancers in the Dark suggested that they felt 'unsupported' by arts organizations and the UK government (Edelman, FitzGibbon and Harris 2021).

Meanwhile, governmentally imposed 50 per cent cuts to arts funding in Higher Education (HE) further signalled a devaluing of arts education amidst the crisis. This followed the reinforcing of other inequalities, including the cancellation of summer exams and the UK government's catastrophic calculation of students' A-level results in

2020 using an AI algorithm widely accused of being biased against students from poorer backgrounds (Kolkman 2020), prompting protest from hundreds of students who chanted 'Fuck the algorithm' outside the UK's Department of Education in August 2020 (*Huck* 2020). Former UK education secretary, Gavin Williamson, claimed that the arts cuts in HE reflected 'priorities that have emerged in the light of the coronavirus pandemic' (Williamson 2021). The argument for de-prioritizing arts subjects is because they were not viewed as vital to the economy and labour markets and not positioned among the government's 'strategic priorities' (Office for Students 2021). However, others speculated that this was an authoritarian top-down attack on dissenting voices within the arts from a government entrenching itself within populist culture wars rhetoric and policies (Wade 2021). Furthermore, the prioritization of *only* that which is perceived to be vital to the economy in national resilience strategies may also explain the widely reported and disproportionate neglect of care homes, with the pandemic-as-glitch making visible the vulnerability of shrinking local government social care budgets since 2010 (Crawford, Stoye and Zaranko 2020, Pocock 2020).

Amidst the crisis for theatre-makers who could not easily show their faces, or share physical space with their audiences without posing a health risk, and against the wider cultural backdrop of devalued arts practices that were especially susceptible to the impacts of the pandemic, in what ways did theatre practices survive and find renewed purpose? In this chapter, we explore adapted forms of online theatre performance, focusing on two examples of Zoom theatre, Coney's *Telephone* and Thaddeus Phillips's collaboration with designer Steven Dufala, *Zoo Motel*. As case studies demonstrating the reflexive survival instinct of theatre-makers continuing their practice from within global quarantines, how did adapted forms of online theatre care for audiences? To what extent might these online experiments recuperate the lost face of Levinas's Other? And can images of others place the same ethical call on us? Mid-pandemic, the 'problem' of face-to-face encounters in lockdown theatres will offer a valuable test-site to examine the wider ethical problems prompted by the mass evacuation to online spaces in remote acts of 'digital care' (discussed in Chapter 4), especially when such encounters are the locus of moral responsibility in Levinasian thought.

The application of Levinas's ethical philosophy to examine theatrical relationships between spectators and performers has not been without issues, even in pre-pandemic times. Nicholas Ridout noted that for Levinas 'the "face" is never any particular face but rather the otherness of the other as it appears to us in the encounter' (2009: 53). But instances of performance necessarily remove the unknowability of 'the' face, since a performance must cast actors and therefore present specific faces marked with ethnicity, age, gender, and so forth. This makes it difficult even for pre-pandemic theatre as a cultural practice to frame the 'Other' in quite the same terms as Levinas's philosophical 'call of the face' proposes. Levinas also expressed reservations about the extent to which the aesthetic realm could provide a space to explore ethics. In 'Reality and Its Shadow' (1948), Levinas was profoundly hostile to aesthetics, where the analysis of theatre and performance is often located. This is because art or 'spectacle' for Levinas offers a reality that is self-enclosed and removed from real-world ethical concreteness (Krassoy 2016), seducing viewers into 'evading responsibility for the world' (Ridout 2009: 55). For this reason, a 'Levinasian turn' in thinking about theatre has necessarily been accompanied by a 'suspicion of the purely aesthetic' and preference for applied and socially engaged performance practices that make claims towards efficacy in terms of social or political change (2009: 56). Even so, scholars of applied theatre such as James Thompson remain cautious about blanket assumptions between caring performance practices and physical co-presence, arguing that it would be naïve to assume that caring for others in our direct physical presence is an inevitability as Levinas's 'call of the face' might imply (Thompson 2020: 41).

Ambivalent otherness: Face ethics mid-lockdown

Levinas is a point of departure in this chapter because face ethics emphasizes an irreconcilable tension mid-pandemic; that while the direct contact associated with interpersonal acts of care posed a health risk, the mitigations to avoid direct face-to-face encounters might lead to moral jeopardy through a Levinasian lens. Consequently, lockdowns prompted a wider discursive turn to face ethics to analyse the moral consequences of the loss of face-to-face interactions. In an online article published towards the beginning of the pandemic, Giles Fraser explores whether Levinas was correct to root morality in face-to-face encounters, questioning 'will the fact that we are conducting so much more of our business with each other through various forms of digital mediation serve to impede or disrupt the moral valence of the face of the other?' (Fraser 2020). Richard Gunderman similarly notes that dealings with faceless others through a Levinasian lens entails 'moral peril' when human beings can be diminished to 'data points' and in aggregate resemble 'nothing more than statistics' (Gunderman 2021).

Offline face-concealing practices such as the wearing of protective masks via Levinasian thought, for Gunderman, 'inevitably' exact a moral and political price. But a problem here is that a pro-Levinasian ethical stance can all too easily become aligned with 'anti-mask' (Birt 2022) and 'anti-quarantine' rhetoric commonly associated with anti-establishment movements such as *Querdenken* ('Thinking Outside the Box') in Germany, or radical grassroots movements peddling conspiracy theories, such as *Hugs Over Masks* in Canada. Anti-mask movements around the world conflated mask mandates in the legitimate interests of public health with 'culture wars' rhetoric of being 'muzzled' and the perception of oppression from 'health dictatorships' (Allemandou 2020). Medical masks, for some, transformed the face of Levinas's Other 'into an object of fear, someone to flee from' (Gavroche 2020).

However, the alignment of anti-mask discourse and Levinasian thought is by no means inevitable. Marie-Aude Baronian argued, by contrast, that in the context of the pandemic the mask reveals the persistent 'frontality of the Other' and instates both 'proximity and distance'. For Baronian, this is not 'proximity akin to the tangible risk of contagion, but the ineluctable confrontation with the Other … Such proximity is thus not to be understood in terms of physical distancing, but, on the contrary, it indicates the social proximity of an Other who is always already distant because the Other is not mastered or appropriated' (2020: 214–15). Through this logic, the migration of masks from the surgical realm to widespread usage in the public sphere does not signal an end to sociality but draws attention to the alterity and unknowable difference of the Other. That said, it's important to recognize that the impacts of mask wearing were experienced differently by different 'Others'. For example, to those with hearing loss for whom facial expressions and lip movements are vital to daily communication (Chodosh, Weinstein and Blustein 2020). Nonetheless, while masks might hinder us from fully recognizing one another and posed an obstacle to communication to circumvent in some cases, they also act as a visible signifier of our collective vulnerability. If the obscuration of the face and/or proximity beyond physical distancing can be read as enhancing alterity, there may be ways to recuperate Levinas's ideas in relation to remote Others online.

With reduced physical contact in quarantine, discursive critical scrutiny of what had become of Levinas's notion of the 'Other' was widespread in online discussions. For Thomas Jacobus de Jong and Carina van de Wetering, totalizing 'crisis discourse' during the pandemic violates the alterity of the Other by identifying them as both 'dangerous' but simultaneously 'in need of protection through corona regulations' (2021: 167). This is reminiscent of the aforementioned claim in Chapter 1 that governmental drives towards 'national resilience' can risk disproportionately casting others as a 'threat' (Weisbrode and Yeung 2020), while growing fears surrounding a potentially threatening 'Other' might relax public views about the use of privacy-encroaching mass surveillance technologies to help contain the virus's spread, as some reports in the UK had suggested (Lewandowsky et al. 2021).[2] We argue that Levinas's conceptualization of an 'Other' is not a given but a site of continued negotiation, especially amidst the impacts of a global pandemic. Mid-pandemic, the public encountered a pervasively ambivalent otherness; Others who might require our protection, while simultaneously posing a risk to our health. And while enhanced state mechanisms of surveillance and control mid-pandemic (e.g. track and trace/contact tracing apps, drone surveillance, vaccine passports etc.) formed part of national 'resilience' strategies, as Sarah Horton had argued, the more the public rely on these mechanisms 'the easier it becomes to regard the Other not as one who summons me to an infinite responsibility but as a vector of disease' (Horton 2021).

A stage for recuperating lost faces?: Lawyer 'cats' and Zoom theatre

With the pivot online mid-lockdown, the widespread emergence of 'Zoom theatre' or 'Zoom plays' enabled disparate quarantined performers and audience members to come together in an online Zoom call, while broadcasting live from multiple distant locations. As a survival reflex, the use of Zoom enabled the continuation and monetization of performance practices to sustain both individuals and institutions mid-pandemic. The mass evacuation to videoconferencing platforms such as Zoom and Microsoft Teams was simultaneously driven by health restrictions and more particularly in relation to live performance, 'the fear and fatality of the public nature of theatre' (Worthen 2021: 195). Zoom theatre in a mid-pandemic context was a stopgap remediation of those aspects of 'theatre' that *could* be remediated to a safer, physically distanced platform online; resembling what Jay Bolter and Richard Grusin referred to as 'retrograde remediation', when newer mediums are absorbed by older ones (1999: 147). However, the sudden shock of the pandemic meant that retrograde remediation in this context entailed primarily drawing on the available affordances of videoconferencing communication amidst rapidly imposed stringent restrictions, rather than a phenomenon led primarily by competition and market forces; Zoom was not designed with 'Zoom theatre' or a 'digital pandemic' in mind.

Zoom theatres might also be said to use the resilience instruments of computer software/hardware to reconcile those bodily and transmissible parts of 'ambivalent others' mid-pandemic that posed the greatest health risk; namely, the respiratory liquid particles that could transmit the virus from an infected person's mouth or nose when coughing, sneezing, speaking, singing or simply breathing. The stigmatization of uninfected people displaying Covid-like symptoms in public was well documented (Williams and Dienes 2020), and the barrier of screens and online interfaces potentially contributed to moving beyond viewing others *only* as 'vectors of disease'. For example, some studies suggested that performing on/through platforms such as Zoom mid-lockdown could be a 'viable communicative and therapeutic activity and an effective strategy for social inclusion' (Karam and Naguib 2022). However, the extent to which the Other of Levinas's face ethics might be recuperated on Zoom is questionable with both the dislocation of 'actual' bodies and mutability of digital bodies through filters, machine learning and other forms of image manipulation. We were minded of one incident that went viral in 2021, in which a lawyer accidentally showed up as a 'cat' avatar to virtual court proceedings on Zoom at the 394th district of Texas, without the technical know-how to be able to switch the filter off ('I'm Not a Cat ...', 2021). On the one hand, this farcical moment demonstrates that shame and humiliation underpinning responsibility in Levinas's ethics are not limited to face-to-face encounters in shared physical space as Levinasian face ethics might imply when interpreted narrowly. But on the other, it offers a stark reminder through the glitching of an online court proceeding of the mediating effect of the medium. Put differently, it is when a technical occurrence stops a medium from being experienced as transparent that the Other's absence is jarringly foregrounded. Here the Zoom caller becomes *more* other than other, to the extent that the lawyer, Rod Ponton, felt compelled to explain to the judge, 'I'm not a cat'. Of greater consequence in an online legal setting is the possibility, either intentionally or unintentionally, of glitches blurring the lines of formal definitions of disobedience, for example, complicating what might conceivably count as 'contempt of court'. According to the Legal Information Institute at Cornell Law School, the purpose of recognizing 'contempt of court' is 'to secure the dignity of the courts and the uninterrupted and unimpeded administration of justice' ('Contempt of Court' 2022). While this moment was recognized as accidental and treated in good humour, identity-concealing filters could serve to complicate the performative ritual of 'dignity' in court and pose an obstruction of a kind.

Slavoj Žižek reached an anti-Levinasian conclusion in 'A Plea for Ethical Violence' (2004) when he noted that while for Levinas the face of the Other breaks the 'vicious circularity of the symbolic order, providing it with the ultimate foundation, the "absolute authenticity"', it becomes a fetish object that '"gentrifies" the terrifying Thing that is the ultimate reality of our neighbour' (Žižek 2004: 5). But there is greater alignment between Levinas and Žižek on the notion that others represented *as* images, avatars or virtual 'stand-ins' reduce them to less demanding 'interface simulacrum' (Žižek 1999). In *Totality and Infinity* (1961) and *Otherwise Than Being* (1974), Levinas argued that the face of the other as an image cannot produce the same ethical call, in part, because representations signal the absence of the very person they depict. But might this concern extend to facial images in human-to-human videoconferencing?

Zoom provides functions that offer agency over other users in ways that are inconceivable face to face, for example, enabling hosts to 'mute' other users, assign them new names/identities or relegate them to a virtual waiting room. Earlier incarnations of Zoom had even enabled hosts to track user's attention levels, unbeknown to them before this function was permanently removed in 2020. Sociologist David Hill examined the connection between avatars and Levinas's discourse on images, arguing that contrary to Levinas's position, online avatars can be endowed with ethical valences (Hill 2013). For Hill, Levinasian ethics can be rehabilitated online 'if we reject his stance that images are not morally provoking', which he does by turning to the aesthetic theories of Aristotle, Hans-Georg Gadamer and Immanuel Kant (2013: 70). But the feeling of responsibility for an Other that an avatar might arouse is contingent for Hill on it being understood as an extension of a *specific person* and *signifying the person that it stands in for*. Returning to the example of the lawyer 'cat' on Zoom, the panic to remove this unwanted avatar might signal that the mismatch between avatar and user had the capacity to diminish their perceived authority/legitimacy, compromise the dignity of the courtroom setting and obfuscate the person that the image should be signposting, and upon which our responsibility towards them might depend, according to Hill.

Zoom theatre could be argued to recuperate something *like* the faces of others to a virtual stage, while having a sanitizing effect on our relations mid-pandemic in the sense of rendering others hygienic, especially when a commonality of all Zoom theatres as a mitigatory artistic practice is that the bodies of others are 'made safe' by their containment. W. B. Worthen argued that 'Zoom theatre claims a kind of medial transparency … to deliver an essentially humanizing experience to its (unfortunately atomized and remote) public', while offering an 'experience of something that's not here, something that may never return [theatre]' (196). Far from 'medial transparency', framing 'Zoom' as a site of 'theatre' brought the absences Worthen alludes to – those things that are *not here* – into sharper relief. Coney's *Telephone* and Thaddeus Phillips's *Zoo Motel* are participatory Zoom performances of different orders that are self-reflexive to this paradox of a 'theatre' that simply cannot arrive.

In the section that follows, we examine Zoom performance events that create spaces to make unlikely and fragile connections with others through compassionate facilitation. In these examples, Zoom hosts remotely engage audiences as other kinds of service providers, from a pseudo-telephone exchange operator in *Telephone*, to the night clerk who checks us in to *Zoo Motel*'s virtual accommodation.

Patching into the past: Coney's *Telephone*

Coney's *Telephone* uses Zoom's functions and reverse-remediates the operations of obsolete communications technologies to celebrate a 'mostly true history' of telecommunications, through a low-fi experience that brings together an intercontinental audience constituent of online 'callers'. Described as a 'gently interactive' work, attendees from around the world meet to re-enact historic communications from the past, including the first phone call in 1876 between Alexander Graham Bell and his assistant Thomas Augustus Watson, and the first text message sent in 1992. Tassos Stevens presents audience members with a directory of numbers with enigmatic titles such as 'Distant Friend' and 'A Moment of Vertigo'.

They choose which number to make a connection to, with Stevens 'patching' them through to intimate public and private stories of human connection across vast distances. Audience members are then invited to share, with strangers in Zoom Breakout Rooms, the story of the first phone calls they can remember making and 'unexpected conversations' that changed their lives (Gillinson 2020). Zoom, in this context, stages chance encounters. It draws on nostalgic communication devices from our pasts, such as rotary dial telephones, as mnemonics for participants to access memories of historic long-distance conversations.

The idea that physical distance is not oppositional to sociality emerges when Stevens alerts his callers to the idea that traversing distance is inherent in the very origins of the word 'telephone', meaning 'distant voice', from the root words *télé* ('far') and *phōnē* ('sound, voice'). Stevens makes the gulf between *Telephone*'s callers visible by inviting them to hold up placards that indicate where they are, spanning locations 3,864 miles apart between Chicago to Kenilworth in the performance I (Liam) attended. Unlike the historic landlines that once anchored callers to a specific location, place is multifaceted and ambiguous in *Telephone*. Stevens highlights this when he says, 'if the Zoom is a room I don't know where it is materially/geographically speaking. Perhaps it's inside a server somewhere in a datafile in the mid-West of the United States. But we're conjuring that we're here together, wherever this "here" is. I guess we're conjuring a theatre.' Neither the 'here' of the performance, nor the different 'theres' of our fellow callers are obvious. For example, in a recording of one performance of *Telephone*, it gradually became apparent that two callers in different Zoom windows were a married couple on different computers in the same physical space. This only became clear when one of them suddenly entered their partner's rectangular Zoom window to recount a shared personal story of their past long-distance relationship. There was an unplanned magic in this telescoping of space akin to Stevens's allusion that we were 'conjuring a theatre'. Stevens also calls upon us to conjure absent others into the gaps of the telecommunications mediums he discusses. In one moment, he reveals an empty office chair behind him, and recounts a Jewish tradition of leaving an empty chair at a feast for the person you wished was there but isn't. He then invites callers to scroll through the contacts on their smartphones and choose someone who is not with them now; he says, 'imagine them sat in the empty chair. You can write a message or imagine writing one – think about what you'll say. Perhaps just that you're thinking about them, and you hope that they are doing okay in this moment. You can send it or imagine sending it'. Stevens invites his callers to consider telephones as a means of summoning, akin to a 'prayerful act'. He recalls reading one of Australian musician Nick Cave's public responses to a fan on the topic in *The Red Hand Files* where he turns agony uncle. Cave says:

> The act of prayer is by no means exclusive to religious practise because prayer is not dependent on the existence of a subject. You need not pray to anyone. It is just as valuable to pray into your disbelief as it is to pray into your belief, for prayer is not an encounter with an external agent, rather it is an encounter with oneself. (Cave 2020)

Unlike Zoom, the faces of Other callers are not images through the medium of a telephone call. They are imagined. This might better coalesce with Levinas's notion that the face in face ethics should not be reduced to a specific face. The other remains elusive, much as the self might become elusive in a prayerful act when encountering oneself *as* 'Other'. Stevens continues, 'The coronavirus has brought us to our knees, yet it has also presented us with the opportunity to be prayerful, whether we believe in god, or not.' Inviting us to re-conjure the imagined friend we had located in the empty office chair, Stevens asks us to now imagine them smiling after receiving our text message that we had previously sent (or imagined sending). The show ends when he says, 'You are thinking about them smiling – and that's actually how the telephone works'. Calling others, like praying, also calls upon the listener to summon aspects of the other that remain distant, imagined and unseen; in doing so, he offers a way of thinking that might offer a frail bridge of comfort in callers' respective grief and isolations.

Lockdown as a hotel room without a door: Thaddeus Phillips's *Zoo Motel*

Zoo Motel – perhaps a wordplay on 'Zoom Hotel' – invited twenty-one audience members participating from around the world via Zoom to 'check-in' to a virtual online hotel. A PDF file is sent in advance to audience members by email as a 'welcome kit', akin to a hotel brochure. This contains a 'room key card' to print out, a map of the hotel and instructions to bring a deck of cards. Participants are greeted in the Zoom 'Waiting Room' by the 'Night Clerk' (Newton Buchanan), who checks us into our rooms and ensures we have everything we need. This greeting, reminiscent of acts of caring from tertiary hospitality service providers in the market economy, arrived at a time when the prospect of travelling, let alone checking into a hotel, seemed impossibly illusory. The ensuing performance was live-streamed from a room in theatre-maker Thaddeus Phillips's family home in Cajicá, Colombia, where he was quarantined mid-pandemic. *Zoo Motel*'s premise is that the central character is a travelling theatre-maker enroute to Spain to direct a play about climate change and 'the end of the world'. His journey is interrupted when he enters his hotel room only to discover that the door behind him has vanished. The metaphor of a doorless room acts as a container for the show and a symbolic expression of our separate yet mutual global confinements. The character reaches out to us as fellow 'guests' of this impossible hotel. The company's stated aim was to make a performance where 'geography does not exist', 'time zones are fluid and global guests can gather in one place', with each visitor isolated in the bubble of 'hotel rooms' that they are invited to imagine adjoin, when the Zoom callers are thousands of miles apart. A central camera pans around the space, as Phillips poetically weaves together seemingly disparate stories of isolation and the desire to make connections across time and space from objects curated in his room, mixing magic illusions, cinematic practical effects such as miniature DIY pop-up sets and storytelling.

Phillips's show, like Coney's *Telephone*, alludes to other historic acts of long-distance communication, referencing Nasa's Golden Records, which were blasted into space aboard the Voyager 1 and 2 probes as a portrait of human life for any alien species that may happen to retrieve them. Like the 'prayerful act' of a phone call, the discs are an as yet one-sided dialogue with the universe directed at unknown and alien otherness; perhaps the ultimate alterity. *Zoo Motel* shares further resonances with Coney's *Telephone*, in the sense that the work seeks to make temporary intercontinental connections via Zoom, deploys tactics to foster a sense of togetherness (such as playing a card trick involving all participants) and references telephones that have connected people across the gulf of different isolations. For example, from a pop-up picture in Phillips's hotel room appears a miniature model of a phone box that was once located in the Mojave Desert (see Figure 2.1). This remote telephone became an internet sensation in

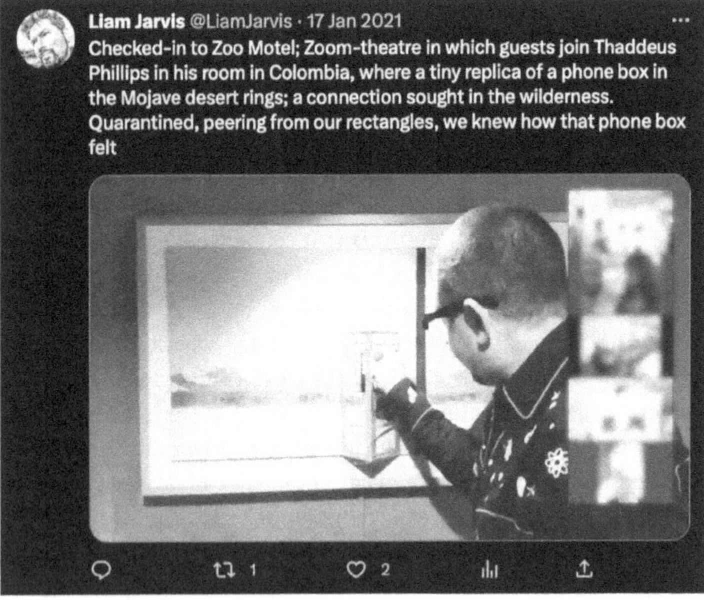

Figure 2.1 Tweet by Liam Jarvis with screenshot of Thaddeus Phillips in *Zoo Motel* (17 January 2021), answering the ringing phone in a pop-up image of a phone box in the Mojave Desert. Tweet © Liam Jarvis, 2021. Screenshot © Thaddeus Phillips, 2021.

1997, with websites featuring it and people calling the number to see who might answer. It even inspired people to travel to its remotest of locations, camp at the site and receive incoming calls from perfect strangers; creating the kinds of chance encounters through prayerfulness that *Telephone* fosters. Eventually, it was removed in the year 2000 at the request of the National Park Service due to the environmental impact visitors were having on the national preserve; a reminder that the desire for humans to connect can simultaneously carry uncaring ecological consequences for the environment. Perhaps even more poignant is Phillips's allusions to the 'wind phone' (風の電話) in Ōtsuchi, Japan; a phone booth like the one in the Mojave Desert, but which houses a disconnected rotary dial phone. It was erected by Itaru Sasaki in his garden after he lost his cousin to cancer. Shortly afterwards, Sasaki's town was devastated by the 2011 tsunami that caused the meltdown of the Fukushima nuclear reactor. In an interview, he reflected that 'there are many people who were not able to say goodbye … families who wish they could have said something at the end, had they known they wouldn't get to speak again' (Sasaki qtd. in Saito 2021). Sasaki decided to open his garden up to visitors who wished to call their deceased loved ones, with thousands making the pilgrimage to this disconnected phone. While extraneous to the content of Phillips's show, it's notable that a Reuters article documents that Sasaki had been approached by organizers who wanted to set up similar phones in Britain and Poland to enable people to 'call relatives they had lost in the coronavirus pandemic' (Saito 2021). Far from a transhumanist desire to 'overcome death' through advancing technologies, here the simple idea was that a non-functioning and increasingly obsolete phone box in a mobile first society could create a much-needed private space to utter unexpressed thoughts and feelings that might be carried on the wind to dead friends and relatives. This was a caring gesture from Sasaki to welcome visitors into his garden and provide a meaningful, if frail, conduit to symbolically 'patch into' lost loved ones.

Loss pervades both *Telephone* and *Zoo Motel*; lost technologies from our past, absent loved ones we might imagine texting, lost opportunities when international travel became impossible for touring theatre-makers mid-pandemic. Both experiences lament the loss of live performance but allude to long-distance communication as a kind of 'magic', hinting at what might be recuperated at the most challenging of times; from the conjuring of a lost theatre in *Telephone* to the invitation from Thaddeus Phillips to imagine an impossible hotel that reconfigured our domestic rooms thousands of miles apart within a single shared Motel building. We encounter only images of the faces of performers and other audience members, but in *Telephone* we connect with chance strangers in a way that the darkened auditorium of many theatre buildings pre-pandemic did not always invite; learning through personal testimonies about phone calls that changed other audience members' lives, and in turn understanding the power of long-distance communication to invoke change. Ironically, it is not the images of faces through the Zoom platform where *Telephone* might be said to recuperate Levinas's face of the Other, but the empty spaces that we can only imagine the other into; the conjuring of the unseeable face of the other caller on the telephone line, or the absent loved one in the empty chair around the table at the feast. Or in *Zoo Motel*, calling into the remotest of locations to make a connection in the desert, or reach a loved one in death. Against the promise of the videoconferencing medium towards 'frictionless' communication, both works express alterity that cannot be collapsed despite the promise of communication technologies to bring the other closer. Levinas's Other is 'always already distant' when they cannot be reduced to the ultimate closeness that is 'I'. And both works play with the paradox of bringing callers together through a medium that instates their separation, while unburdening us from the physical risk we might pose to one another mid-pandemic. To restore engagement with Others, and not 'vectors of disease'.

3
THE SPECTACULARIZATION OF CARE ONLINE

A problem mid-pandemic is that care was easily reduced to a virulent spectacle to provide political expediency for those in power. The semiotics of care could command greater attention than the more sustained, work-intensive and less visible practice of caregiving. This chapter will scrutinize different variations of viral gesturing towards gratitude for the care that others have provided mid-pandemic and the technologies behind the optics. Such spectacles obscure or detract attention from unspectacular realities, such as inadequate support through more substantive but less visible systemic and policy-oriented decision-making.

While deconstructing spectacles of resilience mid-pandemic, we will also locate paradoxes between a desire among the public to show solidarity versus the politicized propagation of 'empty symbols' of spectacular appreciation. More specifically, we examine myriad contradictions of technologies used that were intended to bridge physical distancing in lockdown. The following analysis takes the reader on a trajectory of increasingly distanced encounters, ever further away from the face-to-face on which Levinasian face ethics is predicated. We begin by analyzing direct physical contact, focusing on hospital handshakes from politicians at the early onset of the pandemic, as well as public health messaging around touch. With the introduction of social distancing, we examine the 'Clap for our Carer' phenomenon, which took place at the threshold of people's homes and was initially propagated via social media WhatsApp groups before being hijacked as the governmentally endorsed 'Clap for Heroes'. Finally, we will examine the atomization of crowds through the spectacularization of charity fundraiser Sir Captain Tom Moore using drone swarms to pay tribute as part of socially distanced New Year's celebrations in London. The use of performing drones to commemorate the admirable fundraising efforts of a war veteran and foster a 'war time' spirit against the virus was deeply ambivalent given the ethical concerns about the use of drones to displace labour from jobs performed by humans, to surveil people or to kill distant enemies (Coyne and Hall 2018). We critically interrogate what such symbols of national resilience might be concealing, the ways in which such iconography has been wrested, hijacked or subverted towards different political agendas and the implications of the technologies used in the production of care spectacles.

Performing handshakes: From defiant gestural retail politics to 'bioweapon'

Maria Puig de la Bellacasa argued that to revalue touch is to counter dominant optic regimes that generate disengaged distances with others in the world by claiming to 'see everything by being attached nowhere' (2017: 98). Bellacasa positions touch as a kind of 'caring knowing' when she says, 'like care, touch is called upon not as dominant, but as a neglected mode of relating with compelling potential to restore a gap that keeps knowledge from embracing a fully embodied subjectivity' (2017: 98). But Covid-19 problematized enacting this neglected sense when touching another person became laden with risk. Greetings that were part of everyday life, such as a handshake, were suddenly considered inappropriate or even dangerous. In fields concerned with well-being, the negative psychological impacts of 'touch/skin hunger' or 'touch starvation' were being assessed as a prevalent new form of suffering (Pierce 2020, Durkin 2021). It wasn't just touching people that was risky but touching things. Consumers disinfected their hands before and after shopping, supermarket trolleys were queued up to be disinfected (Kitching 2020) and those most vigilant wiped down their consumer goods when they got back home. Hand sanitizer was stockpiled by panicked consumers, resulting in distilleries such as

Tito's Vodka and Coca Cola rushing to fill the gap in the market for antibacterial handwash.[1] Pandemic restrictions further marginalized the already neglected sense of touch, while amplifying the visual spectacles circulating online.

In the UK, although the spread of the pandemic created a rapidly changing situation, it has been widely documented that a policy of herd immunity was the initial 'resilience' strategy from Boris Johnson's UK government (Peston 2020, Rosen 2021). In a press briefing on 3 March 2020, Johnson had said that the 'coronavirus would not stop him greeting people with a handshake' (Reuters 2020), further boasting that he had shaken hands with 'everybody' at a hospital where infected patients were being treated. This came one day prior to a surge in Covid-19 cases on 4 March (Aspinall 2021) and a day after the Scientific Pandemic Influenza Group on Modelling (SPI-M) had reported projections to the Scientific Advisory Group for Emergencies (SAGE) of a death rate in the UK of between 250,000 and 500,000 people if 'stringent measures' were not imposed (Conn et al. 2020). Despite these mortality rates, fast action wasn't pursued by the government who initially planned to contain the virus through testing and tracing before attempting to delay the peak of infections and subsequently 'mitigation', when further measures were gradually brought in. Notably, by 27 March 2020, Johnson reported that he had himself developed coronavirus symptoms. Meanwhile, across the Atlantic, self-confessedly 'germophobic' President Donald Trump (Lippman 2019) told Fox News at a town hall in early March when coronavirus was spreading in the United States, 'I love the people of this country, and you can't be a politician and not shake hands' (Acosta 2020). Face-to-face encounters in these contexts were not bound up in Levinasian notions of morality with an unknowable Other. This was rather the performance of 'retail politics' in action, which uses face-to-face meetings and 'direct contact' with constituents to feed the spectacle of media by humanizing politicians with the optics of interactivity and community engagement (Trent and Friedenberg 2000). Shaking hands was a self-promoting political gesture, rather than an act of solidarity or attending to the needs of the Other. It might simultaneously be understood as an act of defiance to preserve consumer confidence, maintaining a resilient marketplace and a pre-pandemic status quo in the economy. But underpinning this potentially hazardous display of physical contact was a desire to downplay the prospective impacts of the virus until such a time that the need to impose distancing restrictions made physical contact untenable. A turning point in the UK was a meeting with government officials and members of SAGE on 16 March 2020, when shocking new data modelling suggested an urgent need to change policy to prevent the National Health Service (NHS) from becoming overwhelmed (Morales et al. 2020). In 2021, Johnson's former aide Dominic Cummings alleged that the prime minister had wanted to let Covid-19 'wash through the country' to protect the economy (BBC 2021). 'Others' were conceived of primarily as 'consumers', and not those who may call upon us an 'infinite responsibility' as Levinas had proposed. The initial plan for herd immunization was later abandoned with widespread scientific evidence discrediting this approach (Morens, Folkers and Fauci 2022). But a report from the House of Commons Health and Social Care and Science and Technology Committees criticized the UK government's early approach as 'fatalistic' and prone to 'groupthink', with scientific advisers who weren't open to considering the rigorous approaches to stopping the spread of the virus being adopted in many East and South East Asian countries (House of Commons 2021: 6).

Handshakes with hospital patients underline politicians' initial fatalistic assumptions about the impossibility of suppressing the virus, which exposed the most vulnerable to the already unequal risks posed by Covid-19. Ironically, some historians have speculated that the 'shake' element of a handshake was a motion intended to dislodge hidden weapons up a sleeve (Oxlund 2020), but in the context of a pandemic 'the human hand itself can double as a "bioweapon"' (Garber 2020). By this logic, handshakes had both symbolically and literally become weaponized. Politicians physically connecting with constituents at any cost prioritized feeding the spectacle over the welfare of vulnerable individuals. Thus, spectacles of resilience are part of a scopic regime that prioritizes the image and the economy over sustained acts of interpersonal care. In the subversion of a historical gesture of good faith, handshakes became a power grab to promote herd immunity, enacted by bad faith actors when that very gesture had the known potential to put its hospitalized recipients at risk. It was not until deeper into the pandemic with the rollout of vaccination programmes that the proliferating public spectacle of politicians receiving a vaccination to highlight their public safety displayed a vastly different semiotics of resilience, countering anti-vaccine protests in countries such as France as one of the 'most vaccine-hesitant nations' (Barbero 2020).

Subverting public health messaging: 'Hands, face, back to my place'

Ironically, given Boris Johnson's initial 'resilient' displays of handshaking, in the UK, we were encouraged in the months/years that followed to wash our own hands not just vigorously but patriotically while singing the national anthem for 20 seconds. The UK had recently exited the European Union (so-called Brexit), and some Brexiteers made the argument that freedom from the EU gave the UK more agency to restrict the sharing of vaccine supplies beyond its borders; an idea far removed from the global utilitarian ethics that 'no one is safe until *everyone* is safe'. This insidious link between tribal national interest and the directive to individuals that they might vocalize their patriotism while sanitizing their hands in the bathroom prompted some members of the public to wash their hands to a different tune. Seventeen-year-old William Gibson developed the *Wash Your Lyrics* meme-generator website, which enabled users to create safety posters using either popular song lyrics or their own wording. Bands such as Rage Against the Machine circulated posters generated by the site using the lyrics of their protest song, 'Killing in the Name' (inspired by the Los Angeles riots in 1992). As an ironic nod to the anti-establishment sentiment of the song's chorus, 'Fuck you I won't do what you tell me', the band's poster was accompanied by the message, 'Washing in the name of … On this occasion it's best you do what they tell ya' (Rage Against the Machine [@RATM] 2020). Perversely, this support for a public safety message from a band more commonly associated with anti-authoritarian messaging recuperated their counter-cultural credentials when those in power were caught betraying the very guidelines they imposed on the public. For example, when CCTV footage of UK Health Secretary Matt Hancock's affair with his aide Gina Coladangelo was leaked in May 2021 from inside the Department of Health building, the political message, 'Hands, Face, Space' was soon hijacked to become 'Hands, Face, Back to My Place'. The health secretary was not the only political culprit caught breaking the rules. In January 2022, Prime Minister Boris Johnson apologized to the public for holding parties at No. 10 Downing Street at a time when the country was in lockdown; a scandal that became widely known as 'Partygate'. Images of Johnson in a party hat festooned social media and various greetings cards were being sold with the message, 'Hands, Face, Party at My Place'. The problem with slogans is that they are easily co-opted. What was initially a message of mid-pandemic resilience, putting the responsibility of safety in the 'hands' of the individual, instead highlighted the hypocrisy of political leaders. The crumbling of governmental public health messaging was satirically represented in the montages of Cold War Steve (aka Chris Spencer) – described as 'the Banksy of Twitter' (Mussen 2021) – whose work spectacularized breaches of trust in collages widely disseminated across social media platforms. In one example (*Bluebells*), the unlikely pairing of Dr Harold Shipman – an English general practitioner and serial killer who murdered up to 250 patients under his care – and Matt Hancock, crash a car into a bluebell woodland. Their faces look unfazed by the incident, perhaps a metaphor for a poorly NHS piloted by negligent drivers. Dominic Cummings is positioned at a table from the time he gave a speech in the rose garden at 10 Downing Street, when he had to justify breaking the Covid-19 'stay at home' rules he had contributed to imposing on the public, when he took a trip to Barnard Castle. Meanwhile, Boris Johnson can be seen climbing out of the trunk of the crashed car as the translucent ghosts of elderly Covid-19 victims walk off into the woodland (Cold War Steve [@coldwarsteve] 2020). In an interview, Spencer reflects that while the recurrent inclusion of Shipman in his works represents the 'height of bad taste', especially for the families of his victims, he notes that most of Shipman's 'victims were elderly and vulnerable and our government was contributing to the unnecessary deaths of thousands of vulnerable, elderly people' (Spencer qtd in Mussen 2021). The wresting and remixing of images of politicians into stark new configurations jammed resilience spectacles that constantly projected images of care to evade accountability.

Performing applause: From doorstep clapping to anti-hero worship

Much has been written about the global public displays of gratitude for health workers, carers and other keyworkers mid-pandemic, from the children's pictures of rainbows that adorned the windows of homes (a phenomenon reported across North America, Europe and the UK) to communal rituals of doorstep clapping. 'Clap for Our Carers' was a gesture of appreciation in the UK in which every Thursday at 8 pm from the 26 March 2020, people stood on their doorsteps or leaned from windows to clap or bang pans together in appreciation for the NHS and other keyworkers during the global pandemic. Annemarie Plas is credited with bringing the movement to the UK, having witnessed similar events taking place in Europe via a Dutch WhatsApp group. Other acts of distanced solidarity were emerging in Europe at this time, such as the videos of Italian residents singing the traditional *Canto della Verbena* and *Viva la nostra Siena* from their windows and balconies when Italy imposed the first lockdown on an entire population of any EU nation. Acts of mass applause were heralded by many as a galvanizing ritual of community cohesion but were increasingly critiqued by various commentators as a hollow co-opted gesture that belied frontline services in crisis. One UK survey of health and social care workers indicated that only one-third of respondents overall considered clapping for carers a helpful response (Manthorpe et al. 2021).[2] Where 'heroism' became associated with clapping as a public expression of support, most survey respondents rejected this as a tactic to 'avoid criticism for poor treatment of health and social care staff' (Manthorpe et al. 2021). These kinds of responses may be indicative of why the subsequent attempt to rekindle doorstep clapping, rebranded as 'Clap for Heroes', had failed on 7 January 2021. Plas issued a statement on Twitter just hours before the planned revival of the event to distance herself from it due to 'personal abuse and threats' on social media (Plas 2021). While Plas had not intended to make a 'political statement about the state of the nation', many were developing the impression that the ritual had become 'politicized'. To contextualize these shifting public attitudes, other state-sanctioned symbols of thanks to care workers were emerging, such as Matt Hancock's widely criticized 'badge of honour', which he introduced to allow 'social care staff proudly and publicly to identify themselves' (Clifton 2020) in the weeks that followed the first doorstep clap. The badge was said to offer the social care sector the 'same public recognition as NHS staff', such as priority access to shops in lockdown. But it was widely viewed as a superficial gesture that did little to meaningfully change the fact that social care work had long been undervalued relative to other health and social occupations (Cooke and Bartram 2015). The government piggy-backed the 'Clap for Carers' movement, with Plas being invited to join Boris Johnson outside 10 Downing Street in a collective applaud to mark the seventy-second anniversary of the NHS on 5 July 2020. But this created the optic of official endorsement from the government of a grassroots event previously led by members of the public. Following the announcement of the rebranded 'Clap for Heroes', a counter-initiative led by Jack Monroe sharing the hashtag #ThunderClapforCarers sought to replace clapping with the direct lobbying of MPs to pay essential workers a 'liveable wage'. Meanwhile, many NHS staff publicly rebuked 'hero worship' in favour of adequate pay and appropriate personal protective equipment (PPE). The widespread summoning of war-time imagery in reference to the coronavirus pandemic (aka the 'enemy') was a 'call to arms' for the public, with Hancock claiming, 'we are in a war against an invisible killer' (Hancock 2020). But this 'virus-as-enemy' metaphor became a dangerously flexible target that politicians could add qualifiers to, such as Trump's and other American policymakers' use of the term 'the China virus', prompting a rise in racist anti-Asian attacks in North America (Musu 2020). Similarly, appeals to patriotism presented dangerous implications, as Costanza Musu argued, with political rhetoric casting healthcare professionals and citizens as 'soldiers', implying public 'obedience' rather than public 'awareness' (Musu 2020). Calls to feed the spectacle with heroizing gestures of passive appreciation were met with growing cynicism by many frontline workers. One nurse, Lucy Taylor, told the *Nursing Notes* website that despite the desire to perform appreciation, 'calling us heroes only serves to make it more palatable when one of us dies' (Taylor 2021). Correspondingly, critics were arguing about the importance of shifting 'care gratitude' to 'care justice' (Wood and Skeggs 2020), with arts-based research projects such as China Plate's *#HumansNotHeroes* developing workshops and co-created audio arts projects with healthcare workers from across the UK in collaboration with theatre-makers such as Caroline Horton, Rochi Rampal and Charlotte Bickley. These works, made accessible on SoundCloud, aimed to subvert heroizing media portrayals, raising awareness among the public and policymakers as to the lived experiences of those on the frontline and supporting healthcare workers to find meaning in their experiences.

Resilience optics: Surveillance technologies as care symbols in 'Drone Captain Tom'

At a further remove from the physical touch of handshakes and socially distanced doorstep gesturing was the use of drones. Drones performed various tasks globally during the Covid-19 pandemic, from deploying vaccines and medication to remote and roadless areas in Ghana, Chile and Rwanda (Greenwood 2021) to spraying disinfectants in stadiums, arenas and theatre auditoriums in the United States and Japan (Hershberg 2020). Beyond mid-pandemic usage, drones were also used to kickstart the economy as part of marketing efforts to help local businesses recover from coronavirus-related financial losses when reopening after lockdown. For example, a viral one-shot video of a bowling alley in London used a drone to access 'behind-the-scenes' footage and the inner workings of the automated lanes behind the skittles (Skypower 2021). This demonstrated the capabilities of drone technology to offer unparalleled access and surveil a site in ways unimaginable with human access. More controversially, in terms of infringements on civil liberties mid-pandemic, drones were used by authorities to conduct surveillance on public spaces and to monitor compliance with quarantine restrictions in the UK (Pidd and Dodd 2020), Spain (Steffen 2020), China (D'Amore 2020) and various other nations.

Drones also contributed to the production of public displays of resilience. In 2020, Captain Sir Tom Moore, a war veteran who had served as a British Army officer, made international headlines by raising in the region of £32.8 million for NHS Charities Together by walking 100 laps of his garden in the lead-up to his one-hundredth birthday. Moore's steps were performative in the sense that his gesture accomplished something beyond merely travelling. Each lap acted as a symbolic marker of time to represent a year of his life. But furthermore, every step generated revenue through an online JustGiving fundraising campaign. In a spectacularization of his efforts writ large over the London skyline, The Mayor of London's office commissioned company Skymagic's fleet of 300 drones to depict 'iconic' moments from 2020 as part of a New Year's Eve display (Skymagic), including a raised Black Lives Matter (BLM) fist and Sir Tom's walk (see Figure 3.1). In accordance with 'Tier 4' guidelines at the time, the public were required to stay in their household bubbles, and while no live event took place on New Year's Eve, the pre-recorded drone show was broadcast directly to people's homes. Twitter responses to Sir Tom's image represented by a drone swarm ranged from praise, 'Creating Captain Tom Moore out of drones was genius … but making him wave like that?! So beautiful' (Jackson 2021), to outrage, 'F*cking hell they have done a drone display of Captain Tom Moore. This country is ridiculous' (Ryan 2021). Many tweets used the image as a source for biting satire, with one tweet recognizing the irony of representing an ageing war veteran through military surveillance technologies; 'Tier 6 – Drone Captain Tom hunts you down if you leave the house' (Con. 2021). While another Twitter user shared a mischievously edited version of the image in which Drone Captain Tom's thumbs-up gesture had been replaced by him incongruously 'flipping the bird' at the entire nation below.

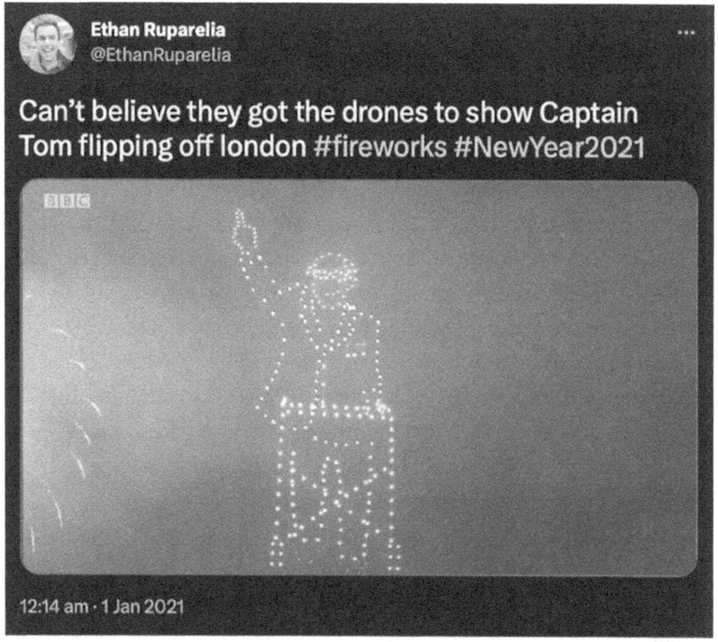

Figure 3.1 Tweet by Ethan Ruparelia (@EthanRuparelia, 1 January 2021) © Ethan Ruparelia, 2021.

The homemade edit of a swearing 'Drone Captain Tom' hijacked an image whose production was already teeming with contradictions. As a spectacle representing Moore's performative act to benefit the NHS, it cost the UK taxpayer and benefitted no one. Political opponents of the mayor decried the spectacle as a 'waste of money', using 'culture wars' imagery for its defiantly pro-EU and BLM 'woke' content. Sir Tom's walk continued to be cynically hijacked as a political prop by the UK government to promote civic responsibility. Drones in a Zimmer frame formation presented the simulacrum of supporting an ageing body, while doing no such thing. 'Drone Captain Tom', unlike the performative garden walk, sought to accomplish nothing. But what was this spectacle of resilience actually propping up?

The use of military technology for entertainment purposes, such as representing a venerated war veteran emblemized as a symbol of national resilience is particularly ethically problematic. Especially considering wider optics around drone usage. For example, in the same month the drone swarm coalesced into a Sir Tom-shaped formation, a UK Ministry of Defence-funded initiative launched twenty drones in the largest military evaluation of the capabilities of swarming drones at that time (Lye 2021). Meanwhile, the US Army's top modernization official, General John Murray, told an audience at the Center for Strategic & International Studies just weeks after London's New Year's drone display that humans may not be able to fight enemy drone swarms, and consequently rules governing human control over artificial intelligence may need to be relaxed (Cox 2021). The proposed relaxation of AI defence technology to counter offensive drone swarms illustrates the increasing removal of human agency, aligned with the problematic evasiveness that's embedded in the root word *resilientia*; the 'fact of avoiding'.

In the wider context of these developments, 'Drone Captain Tom' anthropomorphized and propagandized the very kinds of technologies involved in its image-production, potentially attempting to soften public opinion on drone swarms that have far less 'benevolent' applications. This calls to mind other cultural spectacles, such as Boston Dynamics robots that 'danced' to The Contours' 'Do You Love Me?' in a promotional YouTube video that went viral, presenting the acceptable face of technologies that can be used to more pernicious effects (Boston Dynamics 2020).[3] But in the case of drone swarms, a less benevolent application is that they became a rationale for stepping back human intervention in warfare and promoting the military deployment of AI to counter rapidly advancing enemy threats. Ethicist Mark Coeckelbergh, among many others (Sharkey 2012), has long argued that distancing technologies such as drones used in warfare diminish empathy by removing access to specific knowledge regarding the casualties created (Coeckelbergh 2013). Drones disallow the kind of 'caring knowing' that Bellacasa located in the sense of touch. Furthermore, Mary Manjikian argues that 'drone warriors' are 'unable to behave in an autonomous and agentic way' precisely because of the distance, the obfuscation of moral consequences for their actions and reliance on autonomous technology (Manjikian

2017). For Coeckelbergh, drones clearly violate Levinasian ethical principles. Our duty to the Other and the possibility of autonomous decision-making to exercise mercy are disrupted by removing the encounter with the face of an opponent. For this reason, the use of drones to display symbols of mid-pandemic resilience and care is deeply paradoxical.

'Drone Captain Tom' and wider campaigns to foreground Sir Tom's efforts might also run the danger of promoting the notion that the funding of the NHS is a civic duty, instead of the government's responsibility. Much as Proto-type's opening provocation had flagged concerns about responsibility for care and social welfare being diverted to ill-equipped artists and theatre-makers. The deflection of responsibility for care to charities had long been challenged as far back as the Blind March in 1920 (Sir Captain Tom's birth year), when the National League of the Blind (NLB) protested poor working conditions by holding banners that called for 'social justice not charity' (White 2020). Historically, restrictions in place on health authorities to fundraise for items related to direct patient care were intended to prevent unbalanced service provision between wealthier and poorer regions. But from the 1980s, Margaret Thatcher's government relaxed these restrictions as part of initiatives to promote greater community support for public services. As John Mohan and Bernard Harris have identified, opinion has been divided between using charity for resources, staff and patient comfort and the idea that 'supporting staff wellbeing is a public responsibility, which should include providing decent wages and working conditions without any need for charity'. They further warn that the public's 'commitment to fundraising shouldn't be seen as approval for transferring responsibility from the taxpayer to charity' (Mohan and Harris 2021). The spectacle of Sir Tom's performative walk, heralded as a celebration of civic duty, provided a smokescreen to successive governments' stepping back from responsibility for adequately funded public healthcare provision. This is reaffirmed by a report by the Institute for Public Policy Research (IPPR), which highlighted that the impact of a decade of austerity measures imposed on the NHS after the global financial crisis in 2008 left the health service exposed to 'unnecessary risk' in the wake of the

Covid-19 pandemic (Thomas 2020: 7). This report eschews certain understandings of the word 'resilience' in favour of Seye Abimbola and Stephanie M. Topp's notion of 'adaptation with robustness'; namely, 'the capacity of a system to absorb and recover from shocks and stress without major negative consequences' (Abimbola and Topp 2018).

Handshakes, doorstep clapping and the propagandizing of a war veteran were all optics signalling care while shoring up the UK government's outsourced notion of 'resilience', deferring responsibility to charitable acts by civilians. Retail politics perverted the moral valence of face-to-face encounters to feed the spectacle. And an ageing veteran became a smokescreen to the UK government's 'fact of avoiding' its own direct role in the decline of public welfare and exposure of the health system to shock with 'major negative consequences'. Such criticisms are supported by a damning assessment from the British Medical Association (BMA), which identified that 'chronic neglect of the NHS, poor pandemic preparedness and flawed government policies' contributed to the impact of the Covid-19 crisis in the UK with death rates indicating that the country was one of the hardest hit among comparable nations (Sample 2021). Lurking behind the *Wash Your Lyrics* poster-generator, Cold War Steve's satirical collages and the viral meme of 'Drone Captain Tom' flipping the bird at Twitter users is a desire to subvert the hollow spectacles of resilience theatre. Especially the top-down exploitation of empty signifiers for caring, having conversely imposed over a decade of cuts on the healthcare system (relative to inflation, population growth etc.). A greater distortion than an internet meme imposing an offensive gesture where it did not belong, or the quadcopters disappearing behind Sir Tom's aerial visualization, arguably came from Prime Minister Boris Johnson following Sir Tom's death on 2 February 2021 after contracting coronavirus and pneumonia. Johnson led a national 'clap' in remembrance of Moore's 'heroic' efforts to fund the very health service that the PM's party had systematically defunded. The UK government would later exclude the very nurses they had prompted the public to clap for from a meaningful public sector pay rise, prompting the first walkout in the nursing union's 106-year history (Suleiman and Ferguson 2022). While Sir Tom's performative walk around his garden called upon the public to fundraise for healthcare, the mass walkout of healthcare professionals returned the responsibility back to the UK government. This healthcare strike was an important step in addressing unsustainable pay and poor working conditions as well as realigning the responsibility for care with the government; to show care for those doing the caring. The individual attitude of 'war-time spirit' represented in the actions of Sir Tom were admirable, but this approach also deflected attention from those in government roles who should have done more than spectacularize care.

4
DIGITAL CARE AND PANDEMIC

Maria Puig de la Bellacasa argued that the words 'care', 'caring' and 'carer' are burdened and contested terms, while being common in everyday life (2017: 1). Francesca Cancian and Stacey J. Oliker define care as the 'feelings of affection and responsibility combined with actions [that] provide responsively for an individual's personal needs or well-being, in a face-to-face relationship' (2000: 2). But what of these meanings still apply when care occurs remotely or when the word 'digital' prefixes 'care'? If interpersonal acts of caring take place, as Cancian and Oliker suggest, in a 'face-to-face relationship' – the site of moral valence in Levinasian postmodern ethics – in what ways can care relations manifest when remote access may be all that's available within the isolating restrictions of a global pandemic?

In this chapter, we explore definitions, practices and postdigital divergences with 'digital care'. We also examine tensions when technology had provided remote access to hospitalized Covid-19 patients, but simultaneously kept loved ones at a distance and placed additional emotional labour on healthcare workers. We analyse the personal toll of feeding the spectacle by simultaneously performing care and documenting it in Netflix film *100 Days with Tata* (2021); a film made mid-pandemic by actor Miguel Ángel Muñoz, who captures 100 days living in a tiny flat caring for his great-grandmother's sister, Luisa Cantero ('Tata'). Finally, we seek out resonances in the desire of both arts and healthcare practices mid-pandemic to reclaim the loss of touch. We examine the work of comedian Russell Howard and Nightcap theatre company's *Handle with Care*, which reimagined theatre as care packages sent directly to people's homes. We also look at the caring work and reflective practices of nurses that were active in the Covid-19 wards in hospitals around the world.

Care ethics in post-internet cultures: 'Caring about' and 'caring for'

Care ethics as a field emerged from feminist philosophy in the 1980s through the work of thinkers such as Carol Gilligan, Nel Noddings, Virginia Held, Joan Tronto and Eve Feder Kittay. Theories of care have been applied widely to a variety of performance practices, especially applied and socially engaged practices (Stewart-Fisher and Thompson 2020). We don't intend to replicate that thinking work in this book. However, there are some theoretical concepts from care ethics that can better help us to think through the limits and possibilities of caring 'digitally' or remotely, which will provide foundations for analysing how adapted forms of performance mid-pandemic can 'care' for their audiences.

For Nel Noddings, caring was described as a 'receptive' practice. It entails an engrossment in the other that provides comfort and includes an emotional attachment in the relationship between the one/s caring and the cared-for (1984: 13). Wanting to care can also be accompanied by a feeling of moral obligation, which Noddings defined as 'ethical care'. Theatre companies such as Slung Low (discussed in Chapter 1), who reoriented their practice to prioritize the essential needs of the local community by becoming foodbanks, expressed this type of care as the only way they could 'justify the theatre' (2022: 194). Noddings makes a further distinction between 'caring about' and 'caring for'; a key differentiation is proximity and relationality. We cannot 'care for' all of humanity in the abstract, neither can we easily care for unknown others at a great distance (1999: 36). While Noddings conceded that 'caring about' might provide essential underpinnings for 'caring for', she prioritizes the latter over the former. However, Noddings also acknowledged that caring 'about' may be both foundational to our sense of justice and, on some occasions, the only form of caring available to us. This caveat is especially crucial amidst the restricted access relatives had to hospitalized loved ones mid-pandemic. Reports of the wide-ranging impacts of these restrictions on patients and their families have been well documented by nurses (Correia et al. 2022). The desire to provide face-to-face 'caring-for' had often been untenable because it heightened the risk of transmitting Covid-19 to elderly and vulnerable others. Consequently, the potentials of 'caring about' require critical rethinking in the context of a post-internet pandemic.

'Caring about' expanded: Webs of interdependencies

Caring through different online platforms problematizes Noddings's caring 'about'/'for' binary distinction in a variety of ways. The so-called digital pandemic provided a cultural moment to reflect on our networked interdependencies and the internet provided a space to play out caring needs across an extended web of relations. In *Digital Media, Friendship and Cultures of Care* (2021), Paul Byron considers care as a 'staple element of media life', examining how friendships and intimacies online give shape to and are shaped by the media with which people interact. He argues that 'when we read, scroll and drift through our social media feeds, we are seeing and remembering the people, practices, and things we care about. We scroll because we care' (2021: 2). Others have noted that beyond digital networks, care can be distributed through supporting relations other than human-to-human contact. For example, Judith Butler questions that while those formed within the liberal individualist tradition might understand themselves as 'radically separate' and 'self-standing' individuals, 'who actually stands on their own?' (Butler in Gessen 2020).[1] Butler highlights the assistive technologies and supporting relations provided in the very action of standing up through the affordance of pavements, shoes, orthotics and the care labour from a physical therapist who resides *in* their own walk. For Butler, care resonates through past labours and in present actions and through caringly created material things. We extend this notion to consider the kinds of care that might reside within the design of both adapted forms of socially distanced performance and healthcare practices when relatives were denied physical access to loved ones in Covid-19 wards.

'Caring for' *through* technology, we argue, is feasible within limits – from remote GP appointments to video calls that might have eased another's sense of isolation in lockdown. The internet brings new caring dimensions to the fore, negotiated not only informally between different users but developers of the platforms, including 'caring about' cybersecurity, the managing of other's data/privacy and the amelioration of obstacles to equitable caring exchanges between users, such as uneven technical savviness and unequal access (e.g. through disparities in the competency of different users' hardware etc.). These additional dimensions necessarily expand the tendency of care ethics to focus on 'personal caring encounters' (Stewart-Fisher and Thompson 2020: 13) by taking into consideration users' actions/affordances in the wider online ecologies they participate in, which are, in turn, designed, managed and arbitrated (to varying degrees) by tech companies/corporations. Nonetheless, personal caring encounters *through* technology and between users remain a key aspect of 'digital care'.

What counts as 'digital care'?

'Digital' from the Latin *digitālis* has been described by some theatre scholars as a problematically non-specific concept (Blake 2014: 12), especially when applied to wider 'digital culture'. Etymologically, the word derives from the Latin for 'finger' (*digitus*), articulating discrete units or numerals under ten that could be counted on one's hands. At its most rudimentary, 'digital' in technology pertains to data represented by a series of discrete values (commonly 0 and 1) for electronic storage or processing (*Oxford English Dictionary*). Therefore, care through the portal of digital networks necessarily relays user's data or users *as* information to either one another or dispersed among many users. So, if care might be considered as a caring 'practice' that reflects an individual's 'values' (Held 2006), and 'digital' a computational/informational process, what ethical considerations emerge from 'digital care' as a compound term? Is there any such thing as 'digital care'? Especially, when the very interfaces that relay digital information also obstruct the face-to-face relations on which both Levinas's call of the face and Cancian and Oliker's specific definition of care are predicated.

Much as medical surveillance technologies like endoscopes have long provided visual access to survey organs inside a body, with the suspension of hospital visits mid-pandemic, telecommunications technologies offered vital interpersonal access to hospitalized friends and relatives when safe direct contact became impossible. This included the use of video links to mediate tragic situations, such as end-of-life rituals with vulnerable/elderly Covid-19 patients (Siddique and Marsh 2020). However, adaptive approaches such as this were far from accepted. Analyses of media discourse around mediated forms of bereavement using video links in British online newspaper reports emphasized the insufficiency of these kinds of 'stop-gap' approaches to 'final goodbyes', despite no feasible alternatives (Selman, Sowden and Borgstrom 2021). The primacy given to unmediated face-to-face care in mass media narratives, akin to Levinasian ethics' pre-internet 'call of the face' (at least when interpreted narrowly as face-to-face co-presence in shared physical space), can contribute negatively to those already experiencing loss. This is because they limit the possible narratives around what might be accepted as a 'good death' or 'good grief' in a post-internet pandemic. The pandemic has accelerated the delivery of healthcare through digital platforms and foregrounded issues of how we attend to another's needs online, including through online performances. So it is important to consider what insights care ethics might bring to bear on 'digital care'.

Detached touch: 'Posting about' as 'caring about'?

The word 'finger', at the etymological root of the word 'digital', presented a cruel irony during the pandemic in relation to digital care – digital communication technologies both enabled safe connections and provided a barrier to care through direct touching. Maurice Merleau-Ponty's phenomenology is a common reference point for the notion of the reversibility of touch. That in touching things, we are touched in return. But with the risk of spreading infection came necessary detachment. We became untouchable to those outside of our bubbles. Thomas Dumm discusses two meanings of becoming 'untouchable': firstly, the loss of somebody we care about that makes them untouchable, 'that which we imagine as part of us is separate now' (2008: 132); secondly, to become untouchable ourselves as figures of isolation, 'of absolute loneliness' (2008: 155). The pandemic made many untouchable in both respects, depriving people of the kind of 'caring knowing' bound up in direct contact. Instead, 'posting about' as an alternate mechanism for 'caring about' became a key theme of the pandemic. Politicians, artists, actors and influencers turned to social media and digital platforms, posting updates about mental health, staying safe, working differently and finding alternative platforms to entertain their audiences. This sort of off-staging enabled artists and celebrities to perform their coping and their adapting; to demonstrate resilience and care. What lurked offstage were reminders that 'we are all in this together' through the pull of 'keep looking at me', 'I am still here'. This public sharing from celebrities and artists not only reminded us that the pandemic impacted everyone, but it also provided opportunities for people to be, or continue to be seen, to be known; a proxy for reaching out and touching others.

Care and memory in Miguel Angel Muñoz and Luisa Cantero's *100 Days with Tata*

100 Days with Tata (2021) is a documentary created by Miguel Ángel Muñoz and Luisa Cantero. It offers audiences a shared experience of two people confined to a space, who turn to social media to reach and influence others. But it is also a story of how caring for someone can have both rejuvenating and negative effects. Muñoz is a well-known Spanish actor. He has a very close relationship with his great-grandmother's sister (Cantero), who he calls 'Tata'. In 2016, Muñoz and Tata spent time together making a film, something that celebrated their shared experiences. Tata then suffered a stroke, and when her physical and mental health declined, she needed care during the day and at night. However, when the pandemic started, the carers were no longer willing to come to the house. Tata became untouchable to those who 'cared for' her. Muñoz was concerned that Tata shouldn't be exposed to too many people, as she was already in vulnerable health, so he took the decision to move in with Tata so that he could provide full-time care for her. Alongside the general caring duties of bathing, feeding and administering medicines, Muñoz also found ways to keep Tata stimulated – trying to improve her mental faculties and to find some enjoyment in their confinement. He noticed that several of his colleagues and friends had taken to posting on social media, so he introduced Tata to Instagram (Tata@soylatatareal). They started interacting with people by responding to questions and the public suggested that their social media show should be called '*Cuarentata*'. There are forty-seven videos on Tata's Instagram, and the couple live-streamed several more times. Some involve answering questions from the public, others talking about the past, or dressing up and having fun together. As part of their interaction, they also have a ritual one minute of silence every day to honour those who had died during the pandemic, or for those who hadn't been able to say goodbye to loved ones.

The documentary also captures the doorstep applause for health workers, that had become a weekly ritual across many countries (discussed in Chapter 3). There are many intimate moments captured on camera for the documentary or shared via Tata's Instagram. The show captured audiences of all ages, often with families who watched together. But Tata didn't seem fazed by the attention or impressed by the number of followers she had, though Muñoz says, 'the feedback from all the people following her was very good for her' (52:31). Tata appears as an example of living positively through the pandemic.

With the help of a scriptwriter, Muñoz spent eighteen months shaping the documentary and re-enacting some scenes with Tata. He says he is proud of what they created, as it 'really puts elderly people on the map' (51:36); 'when you reach a certain age you start to vanish … suddenly Tata becomes an influential person' (52:06). Tata talks about how Miguel (Muñoz) makes her happy and how the pains that she had previously suffered went away. She seemed rejuvenated by the experience, and her reactions and responses appeared quicker. Muñoz though suffered from a lack of sleep, reduced energy levels and back pain because of the 24-hour-per-day care he was providing for his great-aunt. After a four-month gap, he resumed therapy online. His therapist explained how Muñoz had given up a lot to look after Tata, and that the impact had been detrimental to his own health. As the lockdown lifted, he encouraged Muñoz to find a new normal: 'I understand it means giving up an image of yourself. The image that you like of yourself giving to others. Narcissism is not love for ourselves, but love for what we want to be, that image that we create of how we'd like to be. You are leaving yourself behind to become the person you wish to be' (1:11:02). These comments from Muñoz's therapist could speak to many who had felt that they'd left something of themselves behind during the pandemic. For some, that was time with those they cared about, lost work that could no longer take place or a sense of loss of their own identity as they adapted to suddenly becoming a carer. However, the comment also recognizes that in falling in love with an image of oneself, one can lose oneself. And escaping images became difficult mid-pandemic when media channels such as Instagram became portals to communicate in the absence of face-to-face contact. The pressure to feed the spectacle with the image of a 'good person' enacting care for Tata put his own health at risk, emphasizing the complex balance between providing care and ensuring the one caring is also cared for. Another celebrity who publicly worked through personal relationships associated with caring practices was UK-based comedian Russell Howard.

Regressing in care: Russell Howard's *Home Time*

In the Netflix limited series *Russell Howard: Lubricant*, the comedian, sitting on his sofa in August 2021, talks about how his recorded documentary was supposed to be a tour in celebration of his stand-up over the past twenty years. The pandemic put paid to those plans and those of Howard's wife, who had scheduled a career break as a doctor to travel with him on his world tour. Howard ended up living with his parents in his childhood bedroom and started communicating with his audiences online. He created a TV show for Sky called *Home Time* in which he talks to other comedians and musicians as well as interviewing healthcare workers. During an interview with Dr Aoife

Abbey, Howard becomes visibly emotional, revealing that Dr Abbey works alongside his wife, who returned to work to support the NHS in crisis. He uses this platform to reach audiences and share his family's personal investment and experience of the pandemic and, as a public figure, he can also bring attention to the caregivers in the NHS. His emotional response resonates both collectively and personally to question the dynamics of care and caring as we previously introduced. On the one hand, as a celebrity with a platform, he can demonstrate that he 'cares about', and on the other, he can reveal how he 'cares for' individuals at the centre of the pandemic.

The special that makes it to Netflix is not the recorded stand-up show but a documentary that edits family memories in archive footage, interviews with Howard and his family and clips from prior stage and screen stand-up. It's an intimate document revealing Howard's relationships, and his insecurities about growing up with those relationships, but it isn't the world tour that he had planned. Instead, Howard takes a tour inward, a regression back to his childhood, both psychologically and literally by staying in his childhood bedroom. The title of the series, *Home Time*, is itself reminiscent of finishing school, aligning the return to one's childhood home at the end of a school day with the government's 'stay-at-home' orders amidst the pandemic.

Miguel Ángel Muñoz with Luisa Cantero (Tata) and Russell Howard, demonstrate the trappings of the stay-at-home orders in place across many countries. For Muñoz and Tata, the experience brought reciprocal joy, both getting to spend quality time together, which had extensive health benefits for Tata, whilst Muñoz's health deteriorated. Howard was isolated from his wife so that she could continue working as a doctor, and not risk spreading the virus, and he chose to use his work to highlight some of these personal struggles. Both examples are projects that have been adapted to make the best of the circumstances: Muñoz and Tata refocus their film to become a documentary of their stay-at-home experience, including creating an Instagram channel, while Howard adapts his tour for television and social media. Although both projects transform care into spectacle, they also share personal enactments of resilience as well as difficulties coping and provide examples of the fluidity between 'caring about' and 'caring for'. As Gretchen Goldman revealed through the tweet of her off-camera messy domestic environment (in Chapter 1), both Howard and Muñoz similarly reveal what is offstage. However, in these examples professional and family responsibilities are merged in the work of the artists, *becoming* the work that is created. Their exposés care *for* others, intimately, and care *about* others through the creation of the work that is disseminated.

The next section examines emerging theatre-makers who have sought to substitute interpersonal care for theatre audiences, bound up in face-to-face encounters in theatre buildings, with self-generating experiences in the isolation of quarantine. Intimacy is created through objects that can be delivered directly to audience members' homes. Scientific studies had shown that while it was possible for people to become infected with SARS-CoV-2 through contact with contaminated surfaces or objects (termed as 'fomites'), the risk was far lower than through exposure to airborne respiratory droplets (Goldman 2020, Baker and Gibson 2022). Consequently, theatre-makers reaching their audiences through deliverable objects was an action that sacrificed some of the familiar components associated with 'in-the-room' live performance to reduce the level of risk posed to others mid-pandemic. But beyond Covid-19 mitigations – and returning to Judith Butler's notion that care labour can continue to reside in *things* (e.g. care through orthotics manifesting in one's walk etc.) – here we analyse how objects mid-pandemic acted as a proxy for missing physical greetings, such as handshakes.

Theatre as care package: Nightcap's *Handle with Care*

A 'performance' that provided resources for self-caring is *Handle with Care* created by Nightcap (Holly Blain-Rodman, Georgina Kirk, Timothy Green, Ines Collado-Diaz and Natasha Wright), a theatre company that emerged from Central School of Speech and Drama's MA Advanced Theatre Practice course. Nightcap envisioned theatre as fifty care packages sent out to their quarantined audience to circumvent the barrier lockdown had posed to accessing theatre buildings. The company expressed that part of the rationale for creating theatre by mail order through the curation of physical objects was their own overexposure to screens in their studies. Notably, online discussion of 'Zoom fatigue' was widespread at this time and the field of science was actively assessing the exhaustion associated with increased video conferencing – for example, using the Zoom Exhaustion and Fatigue Scale (ZEF Scale) to quantitatively measure impacts in psychological studies (Fauville et al. 2021). A scholar in sustainable learning, Gianpiero Petriglieri commented that even when a videoconference call is branded as leisure time, for example, as a 'performance' (as in the examples of *Telephone* and *Zoo Motel* in Chapter 2) or a virtual 'happy hour' spent with colleagues, it is still a 'meeting' because 'mostly we are used to using these tools for work' (qtd. in Jiang 2020). *Handle with Care* dispensed with prevalent communication tools by offering engagement via a nostalgic and tactile medium.

The term 'care package' originates from the humanitarian organization CARE (Cooperative for Assistance and Relief Everywhere), who sent the world's first CARE Packages in 1946 to bring 'humanitarian aid to millions starving in post-war Europe' (Klein 2018). *Handle with Care* was not intended to provide the kind of aid essential for survival, as in the case of Slung Low's foodbank (see Chapter 1). As an aesthetic experience, it is arguable the extent to which it elides with care theorist Daniel Engster's conception of 'caring', which he understood as 'helping individuals to meet their basic needs and to develop and sustain those basic or innate capabilities necessary for survival and basic functioning in society' (2005: 52). However, it provided a way for theatre-makers who were not receiving public funding to respond to the important, if less fundamental, needs of their respective lockdowns, providing prompts to help participants to 'sense', 'feel' and 'imagine', and momentarily counter feelings of isolation and loneliness that were reported as widespread at the time (Ernst et al. 2022). Participants received a 'pre-box' postcard. Handwritten on the card were the words: 'I can't remember the last time I ~~wrote with~~ held a pen and wrote like this' (*Handle with Care* 2020). The significance of crossing out 'wrote with' and replacing it with 'held' is a poignant reminder of both the increasingly obsolete medium of handwritten postcards and nostalgia for the loss of touch. It's a revision that is indicative of a caring act. To be 'held' by and to hold onto something, even an object such as a pen, evokes a sensitivity in writing and receiving the message. Russell Howard relates to this when he says, 'I'm deeply deeply missing stand up … I have a mic that isn't even plugged in, but even holding it, like it … It's something about the coldness of it as well. It just sort of makes sense. You know what I mean? Just holding it there. Just feeling a mic on your chin' (Howard 2021). His description of the object's tactility and temperature sensualizes the way that he feels about communicating with his audiences. The handheld microphone mid-lockdown is reduced to a powerfully functionless symbol. Technology that once amplified his voice to tell jokes to thousands of people in a shared space transformed into a reminder of the lack of direct connection with others. Just as Howard fetishized holding the microphone to reach his audiences, *Handle with Care* approaches the same 'hands on use' significance with the pen.

In the care package sent by Nightcap, disposable medical gloves, in place of 'shaking hands', are the first objects to greet the experiencer. The gloves paradoxically both offer a protective barrier to safeguard against contact/transmission of the virus and provide a symbolic means of locking hands with an absent other by proxy. This symbolic physical connection the experience evokes between the hands of the sender and receiver extends to finding other ways to connect with the forty-nine unseen recipients of these identical care packages. Halfway through the experience, participants are asked to light a candle that is inside the box and place it on their windowsill. They are later asked to email a photo of their lit candle, which joins an ever-growing online repository of all the candles that have been lit by other participants. Each candle offers a connection with unseen others who had shared the experience, while the lighting of candles as a ritual of memorialization almost anticipated the doorstep vigils that would later take place in the UK and around the world. For example, on 23 March 2021, members of the public lit candles as part of the UK National Day of Reflection led by charity Marie Curie to remember those who had died in the pandemic. The gesture of attempting to reclaim lost touch in *Handle with Care*'s medical glove 'handshake' was also replicated in hospitals around the world in critical end-of-life contexts. When patients dying of Covid-19 could not be with their families, members of the nursing team found innovative ways to 'hold the hands' of patients in their last moments when handholding was impossible. One example is a simulation used by two nurses in Sao Carlos, Brazil (see Figure 4.1). Semei Araújo Cunha and Vanessa Formenton improvised the technique they called 'little hands of love' while working in the Santa Felicia Emergency Care Unit. They filled latex medical gloves with warm water in a hospital shower, tying them off like water balloons. 'Cunha demonstrated how she puts the gloves on an unconscious man fighting for his life against COVID-19, placing one glove on each side of the hand. "The patient feels comforted as if someone were holding hands with them", Formenton said' ('Hands of Love' 2021).

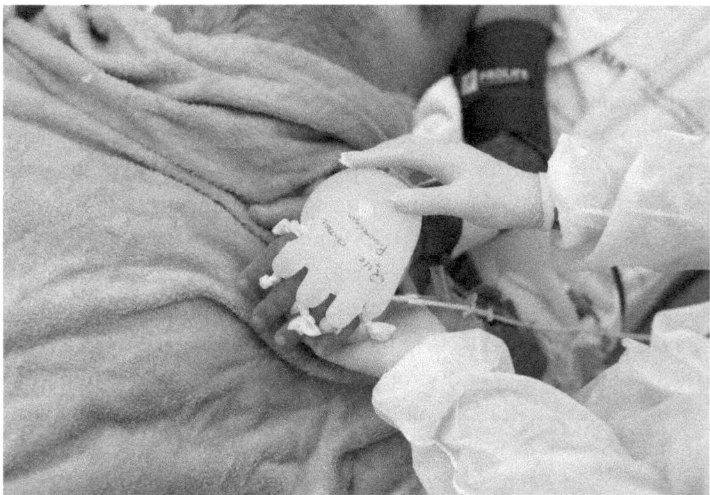

Figure 4.1 Nurse Vanessa Fermenton puts warm water-filled latex gloves that she calls *maozinha do amor* (hands of love) on a Covid-19 patient in Sao Carlos, Brazil. 16 April 2021 (the phrase on the glove reads *Que amor prevaleça* (May love prevail)). © Amanda Perobelli/Reuters Pictures. Reproduced with permission of Reuters Pictures.

This might be a comforting way to approach the issue of lost touch during the pandemic, but how caring can a proxy be for the lost direct presence of a loved one? Helen T. D'Couto, a physician at the Massachusetts General Hospital in the United States, reflects on the ethics of policies that meant Covid-19 patients died alone in hospital. In one instance, she recalls how, with one patient, 'his children kept him company by video on a tablet next to his bed and asked us to hold his cold hand for them' (D'Couto 2022). Although this may have offered some comfort for the patient and the families at home, she questions the necessity of the strict visitor policy: 'the risk of transmission inside an ICU room pales in comparison to the risk of transmission at grocery stores, sporting venues, airports, bars and restaurants' (ibid.). Additionally, the impact of keeping families away from Covid-19 patients in ICUs means that 'families who don't speak English, aren't technology savvy, who don't have powerful connections, or who feel less empowered are often non-white and immigrant families. They are less likely to get exceptions to visitor restrictions' (ibid.).

There is a caring paradox at play here, keeping loved ones apart can cause harm to individuals – patients, caregivers and families – on the other hand it provides the appearance of collective protection. D'Couto says, 'despite a dizzying pace of policy change to keep society going, policies condemning Covid-19 patients to die alone have not changed' (ibid.). In a qualitative descriptive study for the *Journal of Nursing*, Anna Castaldo and colleagues conclude that 'in the absence of families, nurses stood by patients during their last moments, even though this entailed a considerable emotional cost … the consequences are likely to be visible in future years' (2022: 2519). Their study recognizes the role that technology was able to play in enabling communications, and yet the impact on nurses facilitating online interactions was emotionally and psychologically demanding. Nurses would often need to hold the devices, sometimes speak for the patient and would be 'in the room' while intimate, personal and sometimes distraught farewells would be taking place. The nurses' role is explicitly about caring for people, yet the policies that kept families away from dying relatives also caused harm that technological solutions in the so-called 'digital pandemic' could not fully ameliorate.

'Digital care' of this order displaced the complex emotional labour to healthcare workers.

Within Nightcap's care package there is a childhood letter which, like Howard's regression to childhood, provides another tour inward. Sharing stories enabled others to journey somewhere within the confines of their home. In *Handle with Care* the journey is intimate, between individuals, and a sharing of a recollected memory. For nurses at St Cloud hospital in Minnesota, stories were used to heal from the shared trauma of working in Covid-19 wards. Lisa Kilgard, Amanda Shank and Nicole May say, 'writing down how they were feeling was the best way to process these emotions. Amanda noted the healing properties of writing down her trauma, as the nurses in their unit had built up so much stress, emotion and pain, but had nowhere for it to go' ('Healing Words' 2022). Writing the stories took the shape of a book titled *Just Breathe: COVID Stories from the Heart of Minnesota in the Words of Caregivers* (Kilgard, May and Shank 2022). This had a healing process for the authors as well as those reading who had a way of accessing these experiences. However, the stories had the effect of being more than a proxy for the experience, as Kilgard, Shank and May note that 'after reading some of the stories, administrators and lawyers at the hospital volunteered to shadow the nurses, so that they could fully understand what they were reading' (Johnson & Johnson 2022). This understanding could lead to finding and developing new ways of support, and therefore shifting from 'caring about' to 'caring for' nurses, patients and families. Castaldo and others say, 'health-care administrators should provide services that support the emotional and psychological needs of dying people, their loved ones and nurses and plan structural changes in the health-care settings to allow the maintenance of relationships between dying patients and family members' (2022: 2519).

As we have explored, 'digital care' in the context of the pandemic was often a collection of improvisatory stop-gap solutions to restrictions that kept patients from their loved ones, maintaining distance while enabling fragile virtual contact. Where 'digital care' may be problematic is when the term operates primarily to foreground and signpost the intended function of a digital device, as though 'care' might somehow be an inevitable property of its function. Proxies for direct caring were imperfect solutions, from water-filled surgical gloves to extend a relative's touch into spaces where they were denied access, to video links that closed the gap between distant acts of caring 'about' and more direct action associated with caring 'for'. Digital communications also ruptured conceptions of 'good' end-of-life situations. They simultaneously permitted and prevented contact, while the handling and managing of digital devices for dying Covid-19 patients also had the effect of displacing the emotional labour of intimate goodbyes onto healthcare staff already overwhelmed by the scale of the crisis. The lack of support for health professionals at a systemic level means that the care sector could easily be reduced to spectacles of resilience that invited us to passively care 'about', rather than actively 'for', those on the front line – once again, relying on individuals to find a way to overcome the situation; to be individually resilient. But healthcare professionals found innovative collective ways to process their experiences by sharing their stories, while artists and theatre-makers found forms, both through digital circulation and nostalgic care packages, to share work in quarantined audience members' homes. The documenting of acts of caring 'for' provided intimate portraits of the personal toll on artists who became impromptu carers (Muñoz), while touring inwards enabled artists to make regressive journeys to childhood, finding stand-ins to reinstate absent touch as an expression of care.

5 DIGITAL TWINS, AVATARS AND THE METAVERSE

By adapting practices and creating innovative ways to overcome the risks of physical touch, we have seen how artists and health professionals have demonstrated individual resilience. However, as we look to the future it is the development of digital proxies used as representations of 'closeness', 'likeness' and 'sameness' that create more complicated implications for caring and resilience. In this chapter, we explore how the creation of digital twins is an advancement that has implications for autonomy. The development of an embodied internet, or metaverse, is not just an opportunity for expanded infrastructures but creates an additional dynamic for the notion of resilience, which we term 'meta-resilience'. We explore this through two case studies: the Lensa app, which is a digital tool that enables users to create digital doubles, and the creation of South Korean hybrid band, Aespa, whose digital doubles offer constant visibility for marketing purposes and fan engagement. Both examples offer creative opportunities as well as mechanisms for exploitation.

The idea of recreating an embodied identical, a proxy for an original, has already been seen through scientific advancements in cloning, and with digital developments the health sector could find new opportunities in digital twinning. The concept of a 'Digital Twin' (DT) was developed by Michael Grieves in 2002 'based on the idea that a digital informational construct about a physical system could be created as an entity on its own' (Grieves and Vickers 2016). *Forbes* notes that combined with digital twinning, telepresence (a way of being in the same space as someone else using technology) and blockchain (a way of keeping and distributing data safely) converging in the metaverse will have the combined capabilities to enhance healthcare and support patients. Thus, expanding the ways that telemedicine and virtual visits were delivered, and had been essential to the healthcare experience during the pandemic, to develop a more sophisticated and holistic overview of patients' care. *Forbes* announced that with the possibility of creating a digital twin of a patient, illnesses can be predicted and recovery and progress mapped against predictions based on the twin's responses (Marr 2022). With the notion of a DT, we are reminded of sociologist David Hill's idea that avatars can have moral valence if they are linked to someone in the 'real' world (see Chapter 2). However, the creation of a DT carries further questions around alterity. The twin is 'me' but 'not me', created by regular data-sharing from human users so that scenarios can be predicted. In this way, the human and DT are caught in a constant loop where one relies on the input data to understand not only the other, but also one's self. In a study by Bas de Boer and colleagues, there is an invitation for participants to forecast how, regarding health, they would want to interact with a DT. Participants were interested in shifting the current view that healthcare professionals 'are providers of medical information that is passively absorbed by (potential) patients' (de Boer, Strasser and Mulder 2022: 75) to work with the DT as 'coach, diary, back-up, judge, last will, and [health] bank' (2022: 75). In an increasingly strained healthcare system, these types of engagement would enable patients to be 'seen', and to find a more personalized and holistic approach to ongoing healthcare support, mapped across the duration of their life. For this to be effective, there is a requirement for sustained engagement from individuals that puts emphasis on recording data, which could potentially see humans focusing large parts of their energy on trying to predict and prevent health problems, which might cause its own health issues. Additionally, if a DT is a proxy for one's body, and a human engages with the DT in a dynamic way as part of a feedback loop of information and predictions, the distinction between DT and human converges in an ambiguous way. For the DT to provide support that cannot be provided through self-guidance, the DT needs to be accessed and interpreted by others. If the DT is interpreted by others, then the potential for others to 'see' the DT as 'not the patient' could further emphasize the distinctions between 'caring about' and 'caring for' (discussed in Chapter 4). Paradoxically, the potential for others to 'see' the DT *as* the patient also creates an ethical dilemma around ownership. Either way, the DT becomes a new kind of spectacle of resilience that is cared *about* through a spectacle of care, meaning that caring *for* the patient can only be done by the patient themselves.

AI-generated avatars on Lensa

New issues around digital ownership of one's image have arisen, with opportunities for app users to experience their image recreated as AI-generated avatars on the Lensa app.[1] Karen submitted twenty selfie headshots from a variety of angles. It took about an hour to receive one hundred AI-generated images that were thematically organized – such as 'princess', 'pop' and 'anime' (see Figure 5.1). Not all the images looked like 'Karen', whereas others were life-like, and at first seemed 'harmless'. Only head and shoulder selfies had been submitted to the app, yet in one image the AI had created oversized breasts, and in another a body had acquired an extra leg (perhaps the depiction of a leg in movement?). In an article for *Wired*, journalist Olivia Snow reveals disturbing discoveries through her use of the app. Snow deliberately tested the app to check its terms of service around, 'no nudes, no kids,

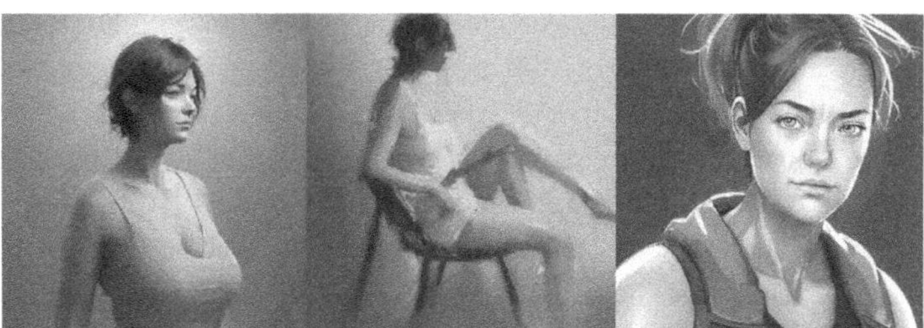

Figure 5.1 AI-generated avatars created on the Lensa app from twenty selfie head shots of Karen Savage © Karen Savage.

adults only' and submitted photos from her childhood: 'What resulted were fully nude photos of an adolescent and sometimes childlike face but a distinctly adult body' (Snow 2022). Melissa Heikkilä reviewed the app for *MIT Technology Review* and reports, 'Lensa's fetish for Asian women is so strong that I got female nudes and sexualized poses even when I directed the app to generate avatars of me as a male' (Heikkilä 2022). Snow reminds us that 'machine-learning algorithms reproduce the cultural biases of both the engineers who code them and the consumers who use them as products' (Snow 2022).

The bias that Snow refers to was evident in the pertinent and widely shared example in 2017 of Twitter user Chukwuemeka Afigbo, a Nigerian technologist who posted a viral tweet of a 'racist' soap dispenser (Afigbo 2017). Afigbo's dark skin could not be registered by the sensors of an automatic dispenser in a public restroom, while Caucasian users' skin was recognized by the device's sensors with little problem. This issue signposted a wider systemic issue concerning a lack of diversity in the industry, which can be built in to the design of a technology or the composition of technologically expedited user experiences. In this instance, it exposed that training data had only been tested on lighter skin.

The ongoing issues with apps, such as Lensa, is that data are required for the machine to learn, but there seems to be little protection in the way that data are uploaded. Furthermore, the fact that the avatar images are created by machines also creates an anonymous author of the image, and removes responsibility, creating opportunity for the images to be mistreated, created inappropriately and recirculated without awareness or agreement. Snow asserts that: 'without any moderation or oversight, the potential for AI-generated violence inherent in "magic avatars" is staggering ... Like most other tech "innovations", Lensa's misuse will most severely harm those already at risk: children, women of color, and sex workers' (Snow 2022).

In the case of Karen's [my] images, these had been selected with care *for* my image, understanding that the interrelational dynamic between what was submitted would produce a version of Karen, avatar Karen. However, the data submitted were treated in a way that didn't care *for* the human user, with app developers only caring *about* the process of machine learning through the creation of avatars rather than the ethical implications of the outputs. This ambiguous relationship between my personal images and those recreated by AI – both 'me' and 'not me', like the ambivalent other of the digital and the complexities between digital twin and human original – leaves me vulnerable in both my 'real' image and my avatar image. Once my image is submitted, there is a lack of control over my representation. What is presented, and what now exists may be convincingly pointing back to 'me', Karen.

Avatar band members in Aespa

During lockdown, a South Korean girl band of four human members and four avatar members was formed by SM Entertainment. Taking advantage of the interrelational dynamic between avatar and human form, Aespa released their debut single in November 2020, bringing a narrative of 'other' worlds to the commercial music scene. The name 'aespa' is 'a combination of "ae", which stands for Avatar X Experience, and "aspect" meaning two-sidedness' (Clark 2021). The combination of real and virtual band members purportedly enables a more interactive relationship between the group and their fans, who they call 'MY', meaning 'most precious friend' ('MY' 2020). Aespa's avatar members engage with MY online, while the human members attend live events. This digital expansion of the group enables them to be more present for their fanbase and opens the dynamic in which the band can be 'seen'. They say it's about 'experiencing a new world via the encounter of the "avatar", your other self' (Kprofiles.com). Creating multiple identities and enacting through them has long been a part of gaming and internet culture and although 'Aespa is an experiment, … it may also be the inevitable next step for the music industry: a fresh way to bridge the virtual and the real' (Bruner 2022). Aespa's approach situates their avatar counterpart alongside their human form in their music videos, photoshoots and interviews, a constant extension of the identity of the band. The merging of avatar with human form is further enhanced by the environment, or avatar world (Kwangya) that is created around them. 'Kwangya' translates to mean the 'wilderness'. It's not only Aespa that refer to this other world, but also a dimension for the existence of a collection of bands, created by SM entertainment and called the SM Culture Universe (SMCU):

> The ambitious initiative is akin to the Marvel Cinematic Universe, which links the various superheroes and villains that fall under its umbrella, and Aespa is at the forefront of this effort. SM chairman Soo-man Lee said the group will 'reflect a future world centered on celebrities and avatars' and represent a 'completely new and innovative group that transcends the boundaries between the real world and the virtual world' (Kim 2021)

The world that Soo-man Lee refers to is a layered fantasy (celebrities and avatars), tantalizing fans through the mist of 'real' encounters and enabled by technology to 'feel real'. However, a 'wilderness' can also be unknown and inhospitable, a place of discovery but also risk. The wilderness may present further risk to the identities of the human band members. Since their avatars point back to themselves, one can question who or what has control? One of the most resounding phrases throughout the pandemic was a call towards the 'new normal'. The SMCU potentially puts a flag in the sand, signifying what, with the development of the metaverse, the 'new normal' for the music performance industry *could* be. The creation of the world surrounding the band is narrated in the lyrics of Aespa's 2022 single, *Girls*. They introduce terms that connect listeners and fans to their world: 'Rekall' is when avatars are in the human world, a 'synk dive' is when the consciousness of avatar and human merge and 'flat' is the place that the avatars live (Irem 2022). The lyrics curiously shift between encounters in real and 'real' worlds, with ambiguous place-making that invites the type of immersion that the metaverse aims and promises to provide. This is further displacing when the human and avatar members of the band explain that 'the more people share their thoughts and feelings, the higher the SYNK level is. When the SYNK level is at its peak, an avatar can REKALL, that is, materialize itself into the real world'

('Synk' 2021). This materializing in the real world is reminiscent of the summoning of an absent other through prayerfulness described in relation to Coney's Zoom performance, *Telephone*, in Chapter 2. It is simultaneously an encounter with oneself and an act of confronting oneself as other.

This crossing over between human and avatar, and materializing from one world to another has obvious traits of science fiction that have played out across various films and TV shows such as *The Matrix* (1999), *Avatar* (2009) and *Sense8* (2015). However, with the development of the metaverse, some of the fiction and fantasy could find a hold in our everyday lives. The summoning of avatar and human into shared space creates an ambiguity around alterity; ownership and responsibility become further confused. Jarvis previously explored these complications in his discussion of virtual property, using the example of a stolen virtual sword in a video game (the 'dragon sabre'). The theft of this digital asset prompted attempts to involve the police which finally resulted in a murder: the 'owner' of the virtual sabre stabbed the thief with a real blade. In the book's conclusion, Jarvis questions 'if virtual objects can have the same ethical significance as physical objects, and a stolen virtual sabre can produce intense feelings of loss, what are the potential consequences of a hijacked body image or avatar?' (2019: 242). We have seen how deepfakes have complicated understandings of 'truth'; how creating a digital image of someone can be used to manipulate or confuse audiences. However, with the creation of a world in which avatars and humans can be summoned across thresholds, there is also potential for further confusion around 'ownership' of one's own body and one's avatar body.

The metaverse

In August 2022, Facebook settled an out-of-court sum to prevent Mark Zuckerberg facing further questioning over the illegal sharing of data with firms such as Cambridge Analytica. The timely rebranding of Facebook to Meta, is, perhaps cynically, an attempt to shake off the bad press of recent years, and to reposition Zuckerberg as the tech-giant leader with a primary interest in people. He says that 'connecting people is in their (company) DNA, and that the metaverse is the next frontier' (Zuckerberg 2021). When Zuckerberg claims that 'connecting people' is Meta's primary goal, it resonates differently compared with Tassos Stevens's claim that *Telephone* is about connecting people. With Stevens, the grassroot message (or 'medium as message') in the work is framed as art; as a space for individuals to participate in a meditation on absence and long-distance communications from within an extant videoconferencing platform. Zuckerberg's emphasis is on monetizing the metaverse. In his Connect 2021 presentation, he says 'think about how many people make a living on the internet today … I expect that the metaverse is going to open up lots of opportunities for people in the exact same way …'. Of course, Meta has its own economic drivers; 'we are investing significantly in building for this future, but the reality is that nobody knows exactly which models are going to work to make this sustainable …'. Zuckerberg continues with a message that on the face of it, might seem collaborative and benevolent: '… we are going to approach this with humility and openness, and we are going to work with anyone whose efforts will help bring the metaverse to life' (2021).

It's widely acknowledged that the pandemic accelerated the development of the metaverse. Researcher Ulubas Hamurcu states that this is largely because of 'the need to overcome the problem of interrupted processes … due to restrictions during the COVID-19 pandemic that prevented people from using the physical environment' (2022: 74). This resonates as a quest or a mission, voiced by Zuckerberg to be an inclusive vision; a collaboration involving '*anyone*', which reminds us of the fantasy world created by Luc Besson in his film *Valerian and The City of a Thousand Planets* (2017). It is based on the French science fiction comic series and set in the twenty-eighth century. The storyline combines themes of war, love, loss, exploration and discovery with visual effects to create multiple species of beings living in several dimensions. There are many species coexisting in the multidimensional universe including the Doghan Daguis, who search for and sell information to other aliens, Mül Converters that can eat and replicate objects multiple times and the Khodar'Khan of which Igon Siruss is a feared Pirate living intradimensionally. It's not a grand leap to align these 'beings' with the mechanisms of the internet, which the development of the metaverse has the potential to heighten; for example, Dhogan Daguis as a personification of data brokering, Mül Converters as replicators of AI-generated images and Igon Siruss as the internet pirate/data thief, or even the online troll.

The high-tech theme is used both in the making of the film and inside the film's narrative. In one sequence, the protagonists visit an augmented reality market. Visitors use virtual reality headwear, while those not wearing the headwear wander around a desert. The scene plays with alternative dimensions and virtual reality encounters that are comical and risky. Laureline comes to Valerian's rescue when his technology fails while trying to escape from a dangerous situation. The juxtaposition of the desert and the dynamic marketplace entices similarities between those who have access, and those who don't, inviting the analysis that without the latest technology, you are literally in the desert. It could also be an invocation of Jean Baudrillard's notion of 'the desert of the real', where hyperreality becomes unhinged from reality and virtual engrossment renders our neglected physical world a wasteland. ITU's statistical analysis shows that 63 per cent of the world's population had access to the internet in 2021. However, 'some 2.9 billion people remain offline, 96 per cent of whom live in developing countries. Those who remain unconnected face multiple barriers, including a lack of access: some 390 million people are not even covered by a mobile broadband signal' (ITU 2021). Meta's call for collaborative action to build the metaverse acknowledges that substantial investments are required across existing infrastructure, but it is not clear what Meta will do to develop infrastructure in the areas currently without basic access. While a third of the world is living in internet poverty, the focus may have shifted from getting *everyone* connected, to getting two-thirds of the world's people *more* connected.

In another scene from the film, Valerian has crashed his ship and Laureline needs to locate him. Instructed by the Doghan Daguis she inserts her head into a jellyfish that can show her what Valerian has seen, but she is warned if she stays inside the jellyfish for longer than a minute then it will begin to feed from her memories. We make a link between the Doghan Daguis's trickster invitation for knowledge (as data brokering), the jellyfish's powers and Meta's invitation for a collaborative metaverse. Access to the metaverse can provide ways of seeing, feeding our experience, but it also becomes a feeder *on* our experiences by consuming our data, hijacking knowledge and profiteering from the encounter. It's no surprise that technology developers want to be at the forefront of monetizing the next steps into a more immersive internet, bridging the gaps between realms that are 'real' with those that 'feel real'. But the issues here are about who and what is at risk for Meta to realize its ambitions. Our interests are not to forecast whether the metaverse will be a success or not, but to acknowledge the energies that are being focused on its development, that are distracting support away from other needs and creating diversions that pose risks for human users and non-users. Meta's statements might sound inspirational: 'almost anything is possible' and 'we will work with anyone'. But within this signalled optimism and lack of selectivity, there is also a lack of care for individuals and the opportunity for misuse and malevolence. Working with 'anyone' to create almost anything can take a rather sinister turn.

CONCLUSION: META-RESILIENCE AND THE 'NEW NORMAL'

Towards the end of his Connect 2021 presentation on the metaverse, Mark Zuckerberg explains how the principles of responsible building need to be embedded from the beginning of its development. He voices that this is a lesson he has 'internalised over the past 5 years' (2021). Cynicism aside, what Zuckerberg is saying that Meta will do is learn from past experiences and build a safer, collectively developed space for social interactions. However, the full impact of developing and interacting in a predominantly virtual social space is not fully known. In the five-year timeframe that Zuckerberg refers to, Facebook was considered to be responsible for enabling a number of online harms, such as the spread of hate speech that incited ethnic violence in Myanmar and Ethiopia (Stecklow 2018, Jackson et al. 2022). We know from experience that risk-free engagement is not possible with large-scale social media interactions, and there is still little development in safeguarding those most vulnerable from abuses of power.[1] Therefore, is it possible to predetermine the social resilience that will be required for engagement with the metaverse? If the tech giants are expressing a desire to collaborate across sectors, then it appears that in order to be meta-resilient one must almost rebuild and understand anew what it is to be social; what it is to be a creator, a participant, and to care about oneself and others in an expanded environment. With experts divided about the progress and direction of technology and the ways that it will be used for building and sustaining a metaverse, it is unlikely that care can or will have the same meaning for all stakeholders. Furthermore, as we have detailed in Chapter 4, 'care' is a burdened and contested term. Therefore, the responsibility for staying safe and being resilient appears to fall to individuals at a time when the pandemic taught us that individual resilience is not always possible.

We understood from Judith Butler's provocation that individuals do not 'stand alone', and in Chapter 5, we introduced the paradox of becoming our own patients using digital twins. In Chapter 1, we explored how theatre buildings/companies had been required to act in other ways, as foodbanks and Nightingale Courts, and in Chapter 4 we discussed how some performance practices found adapted forms of engagement through memory, storytelling and journeying inwards. However, how to care for theatre and audiences through performance practices as we move into expanded spaces will be a creative challenge – one that will likely be embraced by makers, as we have witnessed how performance practices adapt to radically altered circumstances; but the existing infrastructure for theatre will continue to struggle until investment from policymakers and funding bodies catches up with the creative and caring ambitions of the makers.

In 2017, as an agency of the United Nations, the International Telecommunications Union (ITU) launched the Digital Skills for Decent Jobs for Youth Campaign ('Digital Skills Campaign' 2017), and in 2018 they published a toolkit for countries to use to develop a digital strategy. In the UK, the Department for Culture, Media and Sport (DCMS) published a summary of key actions that would need to take place to enhance the digital strategy and reach the sustainable development goals for 2030. DCMS say that 'a thriving digital economy must start with the right foundations' (DCMS 2022). Messages to theatre-makers and artists around funding increasingly require makers to be a significant part of this foundation, pushing responsibility for delivery of the digital strategy onto the arts sector. The Digital Inclusion and Exclusion in the Arts and Cultural Sector report by the Good Things Foundation concludes that

> to ensure that digital delivery remains inclusive over the next decade, it will be important for the arts and cultural sector to understand the potential for new technologies to enhance inclusion, but also the barriers they may raise. For example, an increasing number of people are using smart tech in their home … If the proliferation of these devices leads to an

> increasing amount of arts and cultural content being aimed at these channels, this would have implications for those that don't have access to these technologies, or are unable to use them. (Mackey 2021)

What is lacking from this statement is any consideration to the threat that focusing on building content for individuals to access at home, through their 'smart tech', could have on sustaining theatre and other live practices. In conjunction, many of the actions coming from the UK's Digital Strategy are about delivering access for more of the UK community, including enhancing the current infrastructure with gigabit broadband: 'The coronavirus pandemic has further highlighted the need for widely available and reliable digital connectivity. Around 1.3 million premises do not have a superfast broadband connection available as of September 2021' (Hutton and Baker 2022).

For individuals and organizations working in the arts sector, the considerations that need to be made about the demographic of one's audience, as well as the ambition to expand that audience, can often be at odds with the expectation of funders and policymakers whose aims need to deliver on national and international goals. And therefore situating artists and theatre practitioners within a tide of increasing demands, while needing to prove their adaptability and resilience across multiple agendas. Additionally, the infrastructure for providing individuals, and in some cases, whole communities, with equal or even adequate access to the digital environment is lacking. If, as the latter part of our discussion in this book indicates, a move to a more immersive social environment is prioritized by global tech giants, and the metaverse does manifest all that its architects and designers hope it would (and this is a collective imagination), then the ways that audiences attend, participate and experience live performances will unlikely involve theatre spaces as they have been. A report analysing the impact the pandemic has had on audiences in the east of England, by Rosemary Klich and James Rowson, says that 'audiences haven't yet returned to the spaces they once occupied'. They note that the 'highest percentage of lost audiences is 18–25-year-olds, where 28% of those respondents have not returned to the theatre. The age group with the second highest percentage is the 76+ category, of which 27.6% have not returned' (2022).

The pandemic has shown us that we can adapt when it is necessary, shifting much of our work and social life online, but on the other hand we are comfortable with a 'return to normal'. The metaverse will expand what is normal requiring a new form of resilience, one that embraces the opportunities for hybrid engagements, but also one that understands how to work with the inevitable good and bad 'actors'. Meta-resilience is the wider form of resilience that will need to be acquired for live practices to be sustained. The theatre industry will face challenges as well as opportunities and working collaboratively with other sectors (such as health) to understand safe and inclusive practices will be crucial. Yet, with many sections of the NHS on strike in the UK over pay and working conditions in 2022–3, understanding care and resilience and how we might move from mere spectacle to enacting care and resilience requires systemic change, where our environments, in all the diverse ways that environments are created, are caring for all people and not just for those who hold the power: 'no-one is safe until everyone is safe'. If theatre-makers and artists don't participate in the building of the metaverse then the power will only be held by the tech giants and individuals with deep pockets. Proto-type's provocation at the start of this book said that the pandemic brought us to the brink of change, when the end of the world didn't require too much imagination. And at the same time, the ability to change the power dynamic eluded us. As Chapter 1 explored, at the root of the word 'resilience' is the act of avoidance. A 'new normal' is largely a return to normal, or worse still, a reactive application of the arts to patch over the problems with an under-funded healthcare and social care system that is on its knees, or worse still, 'flat on its face' as UK government opposition have argued.

If the metaverse is to be an extension of our world, then as performance makers and creative practitioners we need to play in the metaverse, so we can have some say over the rules of the game. Simultaneously, the maintaining of both networked and 'off-grid' arts practices that critique the kinds of governmental surveillance that a digital environment might not permit makers to explore (e.g.

through DSMA-Notices or state censorship) will continue to be vital. In a postdigital environment playing in the metaverse may be a recall, a memory of pasts, enabled through the nostalgia of remediated technologies, or performing with our avatar summoned between one platform and the next. The pandemic glitched our working and social practices, disrupting our environments for us to think again about what it is to be a creative practitioner, and what it is to care about and for other people through that practice.

NOTES

1 Spectacles of resilience: Postdigital tensions

1. Controversial appointee David Legates was removed from the White House just months later after publishing controversial papers that questioned the seriousness of climate change without White House approval.
2. For example, higher mortality risks among the elderly, men, those living in deprived areas, minority ethnic groups, and so on.
3. 'Interpandemic' in the World Health Organization's 'Continuum of Pandemic Phases' refers more particularly to the period *pre-* or *post-*pandemic when the global average of cases are at the lowest, whereas the 'alert' phase signals a rise in cases and the 'pandemic' phase represents the period when the greatest global average of cases are occurring. A decrease of cases comes with the 'transition' phase, when spikes or subsequent 'waves' of infection can occur with variants (e.g. delta, omicron variants) until eventually the global average of cases levels out, returning to the 'interpandemic' phase.
4. 'In the criminal justice arena, the 1981 Scarman report was followed by the 1999 MacPherson report, which was followed by the 2017 Lammy report. More recently, there is ongoing evidence of disproportionate stop and search of young black men' (https://www.judiciary.uk/announcements/july-2022-interim-revision-of-the-equal-treatment-bench-book-issued/; date accessed 10 September 2022).
5. 1471 is a number in the UK that telephone users can dial to identify the last telephone number that called.

2 Theatre's 'loss of face': The Levinasian problem of face-to-face encounters mid-pandemic

1. The idiom was originally used by the English trading community in China. The earliest record of 'to lose face' in the sense of reputation originates from J. R. Morrison's *Chinese Commercial Guide* (1834) after the Chinese *diū liǎn* and *diū miànzi*.

2 In the UK, 177 cybersecurity experts signed a 'Joint Statement' voicing concerns about the UK government's initial plan to roll out an NHS contact tracing app that centralized users' data on an external server, rather than keeping processing limited to people's devices (Hamilton 2020).

3 The spectacularization of care online

1 The US Food and Drug Association reinforced stricter guidelines in 2022 for the production of sanitizers. These had previously been relaxed in 2020 to enable companies to respond to consumer demand during the Covid-19 pandemic (Porterfield 2022).

2 Data were drawn from a UK-wide online survey of health and social care workers that was completed between May and July 2020. The survey received 3,425 responses.

3 This video was criticized by James J. Ward, who argued, 'when we allow, celebrate, and laugh at things like this Boston Dynamics video, we're tacitly approving a view of the world where domination and control over pseudo-humans becomes increasingly hard to distinguish from the same desire for domination and control over actual humans' (Ward 2020).

4 Digital care and pandemic

1 Joan Tronto also critiqued neoliberalism's preoccupation with autonomy, attacking the market forces that have reinforced structural inequalities and hierarchies, which relegate care duties to the private realm (Tronto 2013).

5 Digital twins, avatars and the metaverse

1 Since Lensa's download success, there are now a large number of apps claiming to use AI-generated images. For more information, see Sarah Perez's article in *Techcrunch* December 2022.

Conclusion: Meta-resilience and the 'new normal'

1 At the time of writing (December 2022), Andy Burrows continues to advocate for a strengthened Online Safety Bill. He campaigned to introduce this policy in his role as Head of Child Safety Online Policy with the NSPCC during 2017 and 2022.

REFERENCES

100 Days with Tata (2021), [Film] Dir. Miguel Ángel Muñoz, Spain: Netflix.

Abimbola, S., and Topp, S. M. (2018). 'Adaptation with Robustness: The Case for Clarity on the Use of "Resilience" in Health Systems and Global Health'. *BMJ Global Health*, 3.1: e000758.

Acosta, J. (2020). 'Federal Health Officials Would Like Trump to Stop Shaking Hands'. *CNN Politics*. Uploaded 10 March. Accessed 19 December 2021. https://edition.cnn.com/2020/03/10/politics/donald-trump-shaking-hands-coronavirus/index.html.

Afigbo, Chukwuemeka (2017). 'If you have ever had a problem grasping the importance of diversity in tech and its impact on society, watch this video'. *Twitter*. Uploaded 16 August. Accessed 31 January 2022. https://twitter.com/nke_ise/status/897756900753891328?ref_src=twsrc%5Etfw%7Ctwcamp%5Etweetembed%7Ctwterm%5E897756900753891328%7Ctwgr%5Eb270d71b0cfca34f7d578011a8a6a714b5e0e02a%7Ctwcon%5Es1_&ref_url=https%3A%2F%2Fwww.iflscience.com%2Fthis-racist-soap-dispenser-reveals-why-diversity-in-tech-is-muchneeded-43318.

Allemandou, S. (2021). 'France's Anti-maskers: The Faces Behind the Movement'. *France24*. Uploaded 9 October 2021. Accessed 20 December 2021. https://www.france24.com/en/20201009-french-anti-maskers-who-is-behind-this-divergent-movement.

Aspinall, E. (2021). 'COVID-19 Timeline'. British Foreign Policy Group Website. Uploaded 8 April. Accessed 13 November 2021. https://bfpg.co.uk/2020/04/covid-19-timeline/.

Avatar (2009), [Film] Dir. James Cameron. USA: 20th Century Fox.

Baker, C. A., and Gibson, K. E. (2022) 'Persistence of SARS-CoV-2 on Surfaces and Relevance to the Food Industry'. *Current Opinion in Food Science*, 3 June, 47: 100875.

Barbero, M. (2020). 'How France Is Confronting Its Big Anti-vaxx Problem'. *Wired*. Uploaded 17 December. Accessed 20 December 2021. https://www.wired.co.uk/article/france-covid-antivaxx-coronavirus.

Baronian, M-A. (2020). 'Textile-Objects and Alterity: Notes on the Pandemic Mask'. In *Pandemic Media*. Edited by P. Keidl, L. Melamed, V. Hediger and A. Somaini. Accessed 6 December 2022. https://pandemicmedia.

meson.press/wp-content/uploads/2021/02/9783957960092_PM_21-Baronian.pdf.

BBC (2021). 'Covid: Boris Johnson Resisted Autumn Lockdown as Only Over-80s Dying – Dominic Cummings'. Uploaded 20 July. Accessed 12 November 2021. https://www.bbc.co.uk/news/uk-politics-57854811.

Bellacasa, M. P. D. L. (2017). *Matters of Care: Speculative Ethics in More than Human Worlds*. Minneapolis: University of Minnesota Press.

Birt, A. (2022). 'Levinas and Post-Pandemic Masking'. *Philosophy Now* magazine. Accessed 19 November 2022. https://philosophynow.org/issues/151/Levinas_and_Post-Pandemic_Masking.

Blake, B. (2014). *Theatre & the Digital*. London: Bloomsbury.

Bolter, J. D., and Grusin, R. (1999). *Remediation: Understanding New Media*. Cambridge: MIT Press.

Booth, R. (2022). 'Covid Care Home Discharge Policy Was Unlawful, Says Court'. *The Guardian*. Uploaded 27 April. Accessed 11 October 2022. https://www.theguardian.com/world/2022/apr/27/covid-discharging-untested-patients-into-care-homes-was-unlawful-says-court.

Boston Dynamics (2020). 'Do You Love Me?'. YouTube. Uploaded 29 December. Accessed 20 December 2021. https://www.youtube.com/watch?v=fn3KWM1kuAw&t=3s.

Brownlee, D. (2021). 'TRG Arts' Analysis of Performing Arts Box Office Data at One-Year Anniversary of COVID-19 Shutdown Reveals Catastrophic Impact on Both Sides of the Atlantic'. *TRG Arts and Purple Seven*. Uploaded 1 April. Accessed 26 November 2022. https://trgarts.com/blog/benchmark-one-year.html

Bruner, R. (2022). 'How K-Pop Group Aespa Is Making the Metaverse Their Home'. *Time*. Published 11 May. Accessed 13 January 2023. https://time.com/6174945/aespa-2/.

Byron, P. (2021). *Digital Media, Friendship and Cultures of Care*. Abingdon, Oxfordshire: Routledge.

Cabinet Office (2021). 'The National Resilience Strategy: A Call for Evidence'. *Gov.uk*. Accessed 23 December 2021. https://assets.publishing.service.gov.uk/government/uploads/system/uploads/attachment_data/file/1001404/Resilience_Strategy_-_Call_for_Evidence.pdf

Cadwalladr, C. (2019). 'Is This the End of Democracy? #BoFVOICES 2019'. *The Business of Fashion YouTube* channel. Published 21 November. Accessed 12 January 2023. https://www.youtube.com/watch?v=PnYEAMcXIe4.

Cancian, F. M., and Oliker, S. J. (2000). *Caring and Gender*. Walnut Creek, CA: AltaMira Press.

Canning, N., and Robinson, B. (2021). 'Blurring Boundaries: The Invasion of Home as a Safe Space for Families and Children with SEND during

COVID-19 Lockdown in England'. *European Journal of Special Needs Education*, 36.1: 65–79.

Castaldo, A., Lusignani, M., Papini, M., Eleuteri, S., and Matarese, M. (2022). 'Nurses' Experiences of Accompanying Patients Dying During the COVID-19 Pandemic: A Qualitative Descriptive Study'. *Journal of Advanced Nursing*, 78: 2507–21.

Cave, N. (2020). 'A Prayer to Who?'. *The Red Hand Files*. Issue #92, April 2020. Accessed 14 December 2022. https://www.theredhandfiles.com/a-prayer-to-who/.

Chatzichristodoulou, M. (2014). 'Cyberformance? Digital or Networked Performance? Cybertheaters? Virtual Theatres? … Or All of the Above?'. In *Cyposium – the Book*, edited by A. Abrahams and H. Jamieson, 19–30. Brescia: Link Editions.

Chodosh, Joshua, Barbara E. Weinstein and Jan Blustein (2020). 'Face Masks Can Be Devastating for People with Hearing Loss'. *British Medical Journal (BMJ)*. 370: m2683 doi: 10.1136/bmj.m2683.

Chong, W. (2020). 'Online Theater Manifesto'. English version proofread by Tarryn Chun. Uploaded 20 April. Accessed 7 October 2021. https://www.theatrere.org/online-theater-manifesto-in-english.

Clark, I. (2021). 'Glass Speaks to Futuristic K-Pop Group Aespa'. *The Glass Magazine*. Published 12 November. Accessed 4 January 2023. https://www.theglassmagazine.com/glass-interview-with-k-pop-group-aespa.

Clifton, K. (2020). 'Matt Hancock Faces Criticism over New "Badge of Honour" for Social Care Staff'. *Evening Standard*. Uploaded 15 April. Accessed 20 December 2021. https://www.standard.co.uk/news/uk/matt-hancock-badge-honour-social-care-staff-coronavirus-a4415526.html.

Coeckelbergh, M. (2013). 'Drones, Information Technology and Distance: Mapping the Moral Epistemology of Remote Fighting', *Ethics in Technology*, 15.2: 87–98.

Cold War Steve [@coldwarsteve] (2020). 'This ones got bluebells …' [*sic*]. *Twitter*. Uploaded 31 July. Accessed 12 September 2020. https://twitter.com/coldwarsteve/status/1289305917553598469?lang=en.

Con. [@Iamconnaugh] (2021). 'Tier 6 – Drone Captain Tom hunts you down if you leave the house'. *Twitter*. Uploaded 1 January. Accessed 24 February 2021. https://twitter.com/iamconnaugh/status/1344811699380101122?lang=en.

Conn, D., Lawrence, F., Lewis, P., Carrell, S., Pegg, D., Davies, H. and Evans, R. (2020). 'Covid-19 Investigations: Revealed: The Inside Story of the UK's Covid-19 Crisis'. *The Guardian*. Uploaded 29 April. Accessed 20 December 2021. https://www.theguardian.com/world/2020/apr/29/revealed-the-inside-story-of-uk-covid-19-coronavirus-crisis.

Conn, D., and Vinter, R. (2021). 'Liverpool Fan's Death Ruled as 97th of Hillsborough Disaster'. *The Guardian*. Published 28 July. Accessed 2 January 2022. https://www.theguardian.com/football/2021/jul/28/liverpool-fans-death-ruled-as-97th-victim-of-hillsborough-disaster.

Connor, M. (2013). 'What's Postinternet Got to Do with Net Art?'. *Rhizome*. Published 1 November. Accessed 19 December 2022. https://rhizome.org/editorial/2013/nov/01/postinternet/.

'Contempt of Court' (2022). *Legal Information Institute*, Cornell Law School. Last updated in July 2022 by the Wex Definitions Team. Accessed 5 January 2023. https://www.law.cornell.edu/wex/contempt_of_court.

Cooke, F. L., and Bartram, T. (2015). 'Guest Editors' Introduction: Human Resource Management in Health Care and Elderly Care: Current Challenges and Toward a Research Agenda'. *Human Resource Management*, 54: 711–35.

Correia, T. S. P., Martins, M. M., Barroso, F. F., Pinho, L. G., Fonseca, C., Valentim, O. and Lopes, M. (2022). 'The Implications of Family Members' Absence from Hospital Visits during the COVID-19 Pandemic: Nurses' Perceptions'. *International Journal of Environmental Research and Public Health*. Published 24 July, 19.15: 8991. doi: 10.3390/ijerph19158991.

Couldry, N., and Hepp, A. (2016) *The Mediated Construction of Reality*. New York: John Wiley.

Cox, M. (2021). 'To Defeat Enemy Drone Swarms, Troops May Have to Take a Back Seat to Machines, General Says'. *Military.com*. Uploaded 25 January. Accessed 8 November 2021. https://www.military.com/daily-news/2021/01/25/defeat-enemy-drone-swarms-troops-may-have-take-back-seat-machines-general-says.html?utm_source=Sailthru&utm_medium=email&utm_campaign=EBB%2001.26.21&utm_term=Editorial%20-%20Early%20Bird%20Brief.

Coyne, C. J., and Hall, A. R. (2018). 'The Drone Paradox: Fighting Terrorism with Mechanized Terror'. *The Independent Review*, 23.1: 51–67. *JSTOR*, Accessed 31 January 2023. http://www.jstor.org/stable/26591799.

Cramer, F. (2015). 'What Is Post-Digital?' In D. Berry and M. Dieter (eds), *Postdigital Aesthetics: Art, Computation and Design*, 12–27, Basingstoke: Palgrave Macmillan.

Crawford, R., Stoye, G. and Zaranko, B. (2020). 'What Impact Did Cuts to Social Care Spending Have on Hospitals?'. *Institute for Fiscal Studies* website. Published 7 December. Accessed 15 November 2022. https://ifs.org.uk/articles/what-impact-did-cuts-social-care-spending-have-hospitals.

D'Amore, R. (2020). '"Yes, This Drone Is Speaking to You": How China Is Reportedly Enforcing Coronavirus Rules'. *Global News*. Published 11

February. Accessed 13 December 2022. https://globalnews.ca/news/6535353/china-coronavirus-drones-quarantine/.

Davenport, K. (2020) '3 Reasons Why Social Distancing Won't Work for the Theater'. Accessed 26 November 2022. https://kendavenport.com/3-reasons-why-social-distancing-doesnt-work-for-the-theater/.

DCMS (Department for Digital, Culture, Media & Sport) (2022). 'Policy Paper: UK's Digital Strategy'. *Gov.uk*. Published 13 June. Accessed 5 January 2023. https://www.gov.uk/government/publications/uks-digital-strategy.

D'Couto, H. T. (2022). 'Forcing My COVID Patients to Die Alone Is Inhumane – and Unnecessary'. *Wbur*. Published 7 March. Accessed 12 October 2022. https://www.wbur.org/cognoscenti/2022/03/07/covid-patients-icu-dying-alone-helen-t-dcouto.

Debord, G. (1967). *La Societe du Spectacle*. Buchet-Chastel.

De Boer, B., Strasser, C. and Mulder, S. (2022). 'Imagining Digital Twins in Healthcare: Designing for Values as Designing for Technical Milieus'. *Prometheus*, 38.1: 67–81.

Deleuze, G. ([1967] 2004). 'The Method of Dramatization'. In *Desert Islands and Other Texts, 1953–1974*, ed. David Lapoujade, trans. Mike Taormina, 94, Paris: Semiotext(e).

'Digital'. *Oxford English Dictionary*. Accessed 21 September 2021. https://www.oed.com/view/Entry/52611.

'Digital Skills Campaign' (2017). International Telecommunications Union (ITU) and International Labour Organization (ILO). Uploaded 14 June. Accessed 31 January 2023. https://www.decentjobsforyouth.org/commitment/58.

D'Ignazio, C., and Klein, L. (2020). *Data Feminism*. Cambridge: MIT Press.

Dumm, T. (2008). *Loneliness as a Way of Life*. Cambridge, MA: Harvard University Press.

Durkin, J. (2021). '"Touch Hunger": A New Form of Suffering under COVID-19'. *University of New England*. Published 3 March. Accessed 18 October 2022. https://www.une.edu.au/connect/news/2021/03/touch-hunger-causes-new-form-of-suffering-under-covid-19.

Eck, K., and Hatz, S. (2020). 'State Surveillance and the COVID-19 Crisis'. *Journal of Human Rights*, 19.5: 603–12.

Edelman, J., FitzGibbon, A. and Harris, L. (2021). 'Freelancers in the Dark Interim Report #1: The Future from Here: Theatre Freelancers and Planning for the Future during the COVID-19 Pandemic'. *Freelancers in the Dark*. Uploaded May. Accessed 20 December 2021. https://freelancersinthedark.com/the-future-from-here/.

Elleström, L. (2014). *Media Transformation: The Transfer of Media Characteristics among Media*. Houndmills: Palgrave Macmillan.

Engster, D. (2005). 'Rethinking Care Theory: The Practice of Caring and the Obligation to Care'. *Hypatia*, 20.3: 50–74. https://www.cambridge.org/core/journals/hypatia/article/abs/rethinking-care-theory-the-practice-of-caring-and-the-obligation-to-care/BD2558EFE292D5FC57E14016150DB632. Accessed 16 October 2022.

Ernst, M., Niederer, D., Werner, A. M., Czaja, S. J., Mikton, C., Ong, A. D., Rosen, T., Brähler, E. and Beutel, M. E. (2022). 'Loneliness before and during the COVID-19 Pandemic: A Systematic Review with Meta-analysis'. *American Psychologist*, July–August, 77.5: 660–77.

Fauville, G., Luo, M., Queiroz, A. C. M., Bailenson, J. N. and Hancock, J. (2021). 'Zoom Exhaustion & Fatigue Scale'. *Computers in Human Behavior Reports*, 4: 100–19.

Fine, M. (2005). 'Individualization, Risk and the Body: Sociology and Care'. *Journal of Sociology*, Melbourne, 41.3: 247–66.

Fraser, G. (2020). 'What Emmanuel Levinas Would Have to Say about Zoom'. *UnHerd*. Uploaded 30 March. Accessed 6 September 2021. https://unherd.com/thepost/what-emmanuel-levinas-would-have-to-say-about-zoom/.

Freelancers Making Theatre Work (2023). *The Big Freelancer Survey 2023 Report*. Uploaded in June. Accessed 23 June 2023. https://freelancersmaketheatrework.com/wp-content/uploads/2023/06/FMTW-Big-Freelancers-Report-2023.pdf.

Garber, M. (2020). 'Good Riddance to the Handshake: A Terrible Custom Is Gone for Good. Hallelujah'. *The Atlantic*. Uploaded 11 May. Accessed 20 December 2021. https://www.theatlantic.com/culture/archive/2020/05/good-riddance-handshake/611404/.

Gavroche, Julius (2020). 'Losing Face in a Pandemic'. *Autonomies*. Uploaded 16 June. Accessed 6 October 2021. https://autonomies.org/2020/06/__trashed/.

Gessen, M. (2020) 'Judith Butler Wants Us to Reshape Our Rage'. *The New Yorker Interview*. Published 9 February. Accessed 15 December 2022. https://www.newyorker.com/culture/the-new-yorker-interview/judith-butler-wants-us-to-reshape-our-rage.

Gillinson, M. (2020). 'Telephone Review – Dial S for Stranger in a Night of Unexpected Connections'. *The Guardian*. Uploaded 29 June. Accessed 30 September 2022. https://www.theguardian.com/stage/2020/jun/29/telephone-review-coney.

'Glitch'. *Oxford English Dictionary*. Accessed 19 October 2021. Previously published in *A Supplement to the OED*, Volume I (1972). https://www.oed.com/view/Entry/78999?rskey=TIYURV&result=1#eid.

Goldman, E. (2020). 'Exaggerated Risk of Transmission of COVID-19 by Fomites'. *The Lancet Infectious Diseases*, 20 August 2020.8: 892–3.

Goldman, G. [@GretchenTG] (2020). 'Just so I'm being honest'. *Twitter*. Uploaded 15 September. Accessed 27 April 2021. https://twitter.com/gretchentg/status/1305974239984484353?lang=en.

Greenwood, F. (2021). 'Assessing the Impact of Drones in the Global COVID Response', *Brookings* website. Uploaded 30 July. Accessed 6 November 2021. https://www.brookings.edu/techstream/assessing-the-impact-of-drones-in-the-global-covid-response/.

Grieves, M., and Vickers, J. (2016). *Origins of the Digital Twin Concept*. https://www.researchgate.net/publication/307509727. Accessed 2 December 2022.

Gunderman, R. (2021). 'Masking Humanity: Emmanuel Levinas and the Pandemic'. *Law & Liberty*. Uploaded 17 March. Accessed 5 September 2021. https://lawliberty.org/masking-humanity-emmanuel-levinas-and-the-pandemic/.

Hamilton, I. A. (2020). '170 Cybersecurity Experts Warn that British Government's Contact Tracing App Could Be Used to Surveil People even after Coronavirus Has Gone'. *Insider*. Published 29 April. Accessed 13 December 2022. https://www.businessinsider.com/cybersecurity-experts-uk-government-contact-tracing-surveillance-2020-4?r=US&IR=T.

Hancock, M. (2020). 'Controlling the Spread of COVID-19: Health Secretary's Statement to Parliament'. *GOV.UK* website. Published 16 March. Accessed 11 October 2022. https://www.gov.uk/government/speeches/controlling-the-spread-of-covid-19-health-secretarys-statement-to-parliament.

"Hands of Love': Warm Latex Gloves Mimic Human Touch for COVID-19 Patients in Brazil'. *Reuters*. Uploaded 20 April 2021. Accessed 15 August 2022. https://www.reuters.com/world/americas/hands-love-warm-latex-gloves-mimic-human-touch-covid-19-patients-brazil-2021-04-20/.

Haugen, F. (2021). 'Facebook Whistleblower Frances Haugen: The 60 Minutes Interview'. *YouTube*. Uploaded 4 October. Accessed 6 October 2021. https://www.youtube.com/watch?v=_Lx5VmAdZSI&t=202s.

Heikkilä, M. (2022). 'The Viral AI Avatar App Lensa Undressed Me – Without My Consent'. *MIT Technology Review*. Published 12 December. Accessed 22 January 2023. https://www.technologyreview.com/2022/12/12/1064751/the-viral-ai-avatar-app-lensa-undressed-me-without-my-consent/.

Held, V. (2006). *The Ethics of Care: Personal, Political, and Global*. Oxford: Oxford University Press.

Hershberg, M. (2020). 'Company Creates Drones to Disinfect Broadway Theaters'. *Forbes*. Uploaded 19 May. Accessed 6 November 2021. https://

www.forbes.com/sites/marchershberg/2020/05/19/company-creates-drones-to-disinfect-broadway-theaters/?sh=3b9bf5606a38.
Hill, D. (2013). 'Avatar Ethics: Beyond Images and Signs'. *Journal for Cultural Research*, 17.1: 69–84.
HM Courts & Tribunals Service (2020). 'Guidance: Temporary Nightingale Courts and Extra Court Capacity'. *Gov.uk*. Published 3 August. Last updated 5 January 2023. Accessed 7 January 2023. https://www.gov.uk/guidance/courts-and-tribunals-additional-capacity-during-coronavirus-outbreak-nightingale-courts#full-publication-update-history.
Horton, S. (2021). 'When the Face Becomes a Carrier: Biopower, Levinas's Ethics, and Contagion'. *Revista Portuguesa de Filosofia*. 77.2/3: 715–32. JSTOR. Accessed 19 November 2022. https://www.jstor.org/stable/27060124.
House of Commons (Health and Social Care, and Science and Technology Committees) (2021). 'Coronavirus: Lessons Learned to Date: Sixth Report of the Health and Social Care Committee and Third Report of the Science and Technology Committee of Session 2021–22. Published on 12 October. Accessed 3 December 2021. https://committees.parliament.uk/publications/7496/documents/78687/default/.
Howard, R. (2020). [TV Comedy Series]. *Home Time*. Sky One.
Howard, R. (2021). [TV Mini Series]. *Lubricant*. Netflix.
Huck magazine (@HUCKmagazine) (2020). 'Chants of "fuck the algorithm" as a speaker talks of losing her place at medical school because she was downgraded'. *Twitter*. Uploaded 16 August. Accessed 13 November 2022. https://twitter.com/HUCKmagazine/status/1294985562106015750.
Humarcu, H. (2022). 'The Metaverse, Online Communities and (Real) Urban Space'. *Urbani Izziv* 33.2: 73–81.
'Humiliation'. *Oxford English Dictionary*. Accessed 15 October 2021. https://www.oed.com/view/Entry/89368?redirectedFrom=humiliation#eid.
Hutton, G., and Baker, C. (2022). 'Research Briefing: Gigabit-Broadband in the UK: Government Targets and Policy'. *UK Parliament House of Commons Library*. Published 25 February. Accessed 5 January 2023. https://commonslibrary.parliament.uk/research-briefings/cbp-8392/.
'I'm Not a Cat: Lawyer Gets Stuck on Zoom Kitten Filter during Court Case' (2021). *Guardian News*. Uploaded 9 February. Accessed 30 November 2022. https://www.youtube.com/watch?v=lGOofzZOyl8.
Irem (2022). 'Ae-aespa Members Profile & ae Dictionary'. *K Profiles*. Accessed 4 January 2023. https://kprofiles.com/ae-aespa-members-profile-ae-dictionary/.

ITU (2021). 'Internet Uptake Has Accelerated during the Pandemic'. International Telecommunication Union (ITU) website. Accessed 23 February 2023. https://www.itu.int/itu-d/reports/statistics/2021/11/15/internet-use/.

Jackson, Zoe [@ZoeJ311] (2021). 'Creating Captain Tom Moore out of drones was genius … but making him wave like that?! So beautiful'. *Twitter*. Uploaded 1 January. Accessed 24 February 2021. https://twitter.com/ZoeJ311/status/1344803866286698503.

Jackson, J., Kassa, L., Hall, K. and Zelalem, Z. (2022). 'Facebook Accused by Survivors of Letting Activists Incite Ethnic Massacres with Hate and Misinformation in Ethiopia'. *The Bureau of Investigative Journalism*. Published 20 February. Accessed 13 December 2022. https://www.thebureauinvestigates.com/stories/2022-02-20/facebook-accused-of-letting-activists-incite-ethnic-massacres-with-hate-and-misinformation-by-survivors-in-ethiopia.

Jacobus de Jong, T., and Wetering, C. V. D. (2021). 'Welcoming the Other in a Pandemic Society'. *Netherlands Journal of Legal Philosophy*, 50.2: 151–67.

Jarvis, L. (2019). *Immersive Embodiment: Theatres of Mislocalized Sensation*. Palgrave Macmillan.

Jarvis, L., and Savage, K. (2021). *Avatars, Activism and Postdigital Performance: Precarious Intermedial Identities*. London: Bloomsbury Methuen.

Jiang, M. (2020). 'The Reason Zoom Calls Drain Your Energy'. *BBC Remote Control*. Uploaded 22 April. Accessed 16 September 2020. Available at: https://www.bbc.com/worklife/article/20200421-why-zoom-video-chats-are-so-exhausting.

Johnson & Johnson (2022). 'Healing Words: How Nurses in One Covid-19 Unit Found an Innovative Approach to Dealing With Trauma'. Accessed 12 June 2022. https://nursing.jnj.com/nursing-news-events/nurses-leading-innovation/healing-words-how-nurses-in-one-covid-19-unit-found-an-innovative-approach-to-dealing-with-trauma.

Judicial College (2021). *Equal Treatment Bench Book*. February 2021 edition (July 2022 revision). https://www.judiciary.uk/wp-content/uploads/2022/09/Equal_Treatment_Bench_Book_July_2022_revision.pdf.

Jurgenson, Nathan (2011). 'Digital Dualism and the Fallacy of Web Objectivity'. *Cyborgology*. Published 13 September. Accessed 20 April 2023. https://thesocietypages.org/cyborgology/2011/09/13/digital-dualism-and-the-fallacy-of-web-objectivity/.

Karam, K. M., and Naguib, G. M. (2022). 'The Potentials and Challenges of Zoom Live Theatre during Coronavirus Lockdown: Pandemic Therapy and Corona Chicken (Part Two)'. *New Theatre Quarterly*, 38.2: 151–71.

Published online by Cambridge University Press: 20 April. Accessed 26 November 2022. https://www.cambridge.org/core/journals/new-theatre-quarterly/article/potentials-and-challenges-of-zoom-live-theatre-during-coronavirus-lockdown-pandemic-therapy-and-corona-chicken-part-two/38345A2107D26FABFF6A11C7FC401AD4.

Kilgard, L., May, N. and Shank, A. (2022). *Just Breathe: COVID Stories from the Heart of Minnesota in the Words of Caregivers*. St. Cloud, MN: Rengel Printing.

Kim, R. (2021). 'Aespa's "Savage" Science Fiction'. *MTV News*. Published 7 October. Accessed 4 January 2023. https://www.mtv.com/news/xd7x51/aespa-ai-savage-interview.

Kitching, C. (2020). 'Coronavirus: Costco Staff Disinfecting Trolley Handles as Shoppers Enter Store'. *Mirror*. Published 6 March. Accessed 15 November 2022. https://www.mirror.co.uk/news/uk-news/coronavirus-costco-staff-disinfecting-trolley-21643723.

Klein, C. (2018). 'The First CARE Package'. *History*. Published 30 August. Accessed 11 January 2021. https://www.history.com/news/the-first-care-package.

Klich, R., and Rowson, J. (2022). 'Theatres beyond the Stage: The Recovery of Regional Theatres as Placemakers in the East of England'. Project Report. University of Essex.

Kolkman, D. (2020). '"F**k the Algorithm"?: What the World Can Learn from the UK's A-Level Grading Fiasco'. *London School of Economics Blog*. Uploaded 26 August. Accessed 13 November 2022. https://blogs.lse.ac.uk/impactofsocialsciences/2020/08/26/fk-the-algorithm-what-the-world-can-learn-from-the-uks-a-level-grading-fiasco/.

Krassoy, A. (2016). 'The Ethics of the Face in Art: On the Margins of Levinas's Theory of Ethical Signification in Art', *Estetika: The Central European Journal of Aesthetics*, 53.1: 42–73.

Lanceley, M. (2021). 'Lowry Hillsborough Disaster Trial Collapses as Judge Rules No Case to Answer'. *Salford Now*. Published 26 May. Accessed 9 September 2022. http://www.salfordnow.co.uk/2021/05/26/lowry-hillsborough-disaster-trial-collapses-as-judge-rules-no-case-to-answer/.

Lane, A. (2022). *The Club on the Edge of Town: A Pandemic Memoir*. Salamander Street.

Lavender, A. (2017). 'The Internet, Theatre, and Time: Transmediating the Theatron'. *Contemporary Theatre Review*, 27.3: 340–52.

Levinas, E. ([1948]1989). 'Reality and Its Shadow'. In *The Levinas Reader*, ed. S. Hand, 129–43. Oxford: Blackwell Publishers.

Levinas, Emmanuel (1961). *Totality and Infinity: An Essay on Exteriority*. Translated by Alphonso Lingis. Pittsburgh, PA: Duquesne University Press.

Levinas, E. (1969). *Totality and Infinity: An Essay on Exteriority*. Translated by Alphonso Lingis. Pittsburgh, PA: Duquesne University Press.

Levinas, E. (2003). *On Escape. De l'évasion*. Translated by Bettina Bergo. Stanford, CA: Stanford University Press.

Levinas, E. ([1974] 2008). *Otherwise than Being or Beyond Essence*. Translated by Alphonso Lingis. Pittsburgh, PA: Duquesne University Press.

Lewandowsky, S., Dennis, S., Perfors, A., Kashima, Y., White, J. P., Garrett, P., Little. D. R. and Yesilada, M. (2021). 'Public Acceptance of Privacy-Encroaching Policies to Address the COVID-19 Pandemic in the United Kingdom'. *PLoS One*. Published 22 January. Accessed 20 November 2022. https://journals.plos.org/plosone/article?id=10.1371/journal.pone.0245740.

Lippman, D. (2019). 'The Purell Presidency: Trump Aides Learn the President's Real Red Line'. *Politico*. Uploaded 7 July. Accessed 20 December 2021. https://www.politico.com/story/2019/07/07/donald-trump-germaphobe-1399258.

Lye, H. (2021). 'UK Flies 20-Drone Swarm in Major Test'. *Airforce Technology*. Uploaded 28 January (Updated 5 February 2021). Accessed 8 November 2021. https://www.airforce-technology.com/news/uk-flies-20-drone-swarm-in-major-test/.

MacKenzie, I., and Porter, R. (2011). 'Dramatization as Method in Political Theory'. *Contemporary Political Theory*, 10: 482–501. Uploaded 19 July 2011. Accessed 17 August 2022. https://link.springer.com/article/10.1057/cpt.2010.38.

Mackey, J. (2021). 'Digital Inclusion and Exclusion in the Arts and Cultural Sector report'. Good Things Foundation, by Jane Mackey. Published July. Accessed 31 January 2023. https://www.artscouncil.org.uk/sites/default/files/downloadfile/Good_Things_Foundation_Arts_Council_Report.pdf.

Manjikian, M. (2017). *A Typology of Arguments about Drone Ethics*. US Army War College: USAWC Press. Accessed 31 January 2023. https://press.armywarcollege.edu/cgi/viewcontent.cgi?article=1287&context=monographs.

Manthorpe, J., Iliffe, S., Gillen, P., Moriarty, J., Mallett, J., Schroder, H., Currie, D., Jermaine Ravalier, J. and McFadden, P. (2021). 'Clapping for Carers in the Covid-19 Crisis: Carers' Reflections in a UK Survey'. *Health and Social Care in the Community*. Published 14 June. Accessed 3 December 2021. https://onlinelibrary.wiley.com/doi/full/10.1111/hsc.13474.

Marr, B. (2022). 'The Amazing Possibilities of Healthcare in the Metaverse'. Forbes. Published 23 February. Accessed 4 January 2023. https://www.for

bes.com/sites/bernardmarr/2022/02/23/the-amazing-possibilities-of-healthcare-in-the-metaverse/.

Masterson, G. [@GuyMasterson] (2020). 'From a friend: "I have it on good authority that at a Zoom meeting about the future of the Arts with Downing Street, Cummings told Sam Mendes that he wasn't interested and that: 'the fucking ballerinas can get to the back of the queue'" … @BorisJohnson what have you to say?'. *Twitter*. Uploaded 2 August 2020. Accessed 27 December 2021. https://twitter.com/GuyMasterson/status/1290053942064418822.

The Matrix (1999). [Film] Dir. The Wachowskis. Warner Bros. Entertainment.

Mohan, J., and Harris, B. (2021). 'After the Death of Captain Sir Tom Moore, What Role Should Charity Play in Funding the NHS?'. *The Conversation*. Uploaded 25 February. Accessed 8 November 2021. https://theconversation.com/after-the-death-of-captain-sir-tom-moore-what-role-should-charity-play-in-funding-the-nhs-154693.

Mol, A. M. (2008). *The Logic of Care: Health and the Problem of Patient Choice*. New York: Routledge.

Morales, A., Ring, S., Hutton, R. and Paton, J. (2020). 'How the Alarm Went Off Too Late in Britain's Virus Response'. *Bloomberg*. Uploaded 24 April. Accessed 3 December 2021. https://www.bloomberg.com/news/features/2020-04-24/coronavirus-uk-how-boris-johnson-s-government-let-virus-get-away.

Morens, D. M., Folkers, G. K. and Fauci, A. S. (2022). 'The Concept of Classical Herd Immunity May Not Apply to COVID-19'. *Journal of Infectious Diseases*, 226.2: 195–8.

Mussen, M. (2021). 'Cold War Steve: How the Banksy of Twitter Turned Covid Angst Into Art'. *Joe.co.uk*. Published 20 October. Accessed 2 February 2022. https://www.joe.co.uk/news/cold-war-steve-how-the-banksy-of-twitter-turned-covid-angst-into-art-294820.

Musu, C. (2020). 'War Metaphors Used for COVID-19 Are Compelling but also Dangerous'. *The Conversation*. Uploaded 8 April. Accessed 20 December 2021. https://theconversation.com/war-metaphors-used-for-covid-19-are-compelling-but-also-dangerous-135406.

'MY' (2020). *Aespa Wiki*. Published 16 November. Accessed 13 January 2023. https://aespa.fandom.com/wiki/MY.

Nightingale, F. (1946). *Notes on Nursing: What It Is, and What It Is Not*. Philadelphia, PA: J.B. Lippincott.

Noddings, N. (1984). *Caring: A Feminine Approach to Ethics and Moral Education*. Berkeley: University of California Press.

Noddings, N. (1999). 'Two Concepts of Caring', *Philosophy of Education*. Accessed 1 December 2020. https://educationjournal.web.illinois.edu/archive/index.php/pes/article/view/2024.pdf.

Office for Students (2021). 'Consultation on Recurrent Funding for 2021–22'. *Office for Students* website. Uploaded 26 March. Accessed 13 November 2022. https://www.officeforstudents.org.uk/media/8610a7a4-0ae3-47d3-9129-f234e086c43c/consultation-on-funding-for-ay2021-22-finalforweb.pdf.

Okano-Heijmans, M. (2020). 'Coronavirus: The World's First Digital Pandemic'. *Clingendael*. Uploaded 26 March. Accessed 24 October 2022. https://www.clingendael.org/publication/coronavirus-worlds-first-digital-pandemic.

Oxlund, B. (2020). 'An Anthropology of the Handshake'. *Anthropology Now*, 12.1: 39–44. Published 25 June. Accessed 20 December 2022.

Papagiannouli, C. (2011). 'Cyberformance and the Cyberstage'. *International Journal of the Arts in Society*, 6.4: 273–82.

Pérez, E. (2014). 'Meaningful Connections: Exploring the Uses of Telematic Technology in Performance'. *Liminalities – A Journal of Performance Studies*, 10.1. http://liminalities.net/10-1/meaningful-connections.pdf.

Perez, S. (2022). 'AI Art Apps Are Cluttering the App Store's Top Charts Following Lensa AI's Success'. *TechCrunch*. Accessed 12 January 2023. https://techcrunch.com/2022/12/12/ai-art-apps-are-cluttering-the-app-stores-top-charts-following-lensa-ais-success/.

Peston, R. (2020). '"Herd Immunity" Will Be Vital to Stopping Coronavirus'. *The Spectator*. Uploaded 12 March. Accessed 3 December 2021. https://www.spectator.co.uk/article/Herd-immunity--will-be-vital-to-stopping-coronavirus

Pidd, H., and Dodd, V. (2020). 'UK Police Use Drones and Roadblocks to Enforce Lockdown'. *Guardian*. Uploaded 26 March. Accessed 6 November 2021. https://www.theguardian.com/world/2020/mar/26/uk-police-use-drones-and-roadblocks-to-enforce-lockdown.

Pierce, S. (2020). 'Touch Starvation Is a Consequence of COVID-19's Physical Distancing'. *Texas Medical Centre*. Uploaded 15 May 2022. Accessed 18 October 2022. https://www.tmc.edu/news/2020/05/touch-starvation/.

Plas, A. (2021). 'Official Statement from the Founder of #ClapForOurCarers' and #ClapForHeroes'. Twitter: @ClapforheroesUK. Uploaded 7 January 2021. Accessed 16 November 2022. https://twitter.com/Clapforheroesuk/status/1347187352867897344.

Platt, L., and Warwick, R. (2020). 'Are Some Ethnic Groups More Vulnerable to COVID-19 than Others?'. *The Institute for Fiscal Studies*. Uploaded May. Accessed 7 October 2021. https://ifs.org.uk/inequality/

wp-content/uploads/2020/04/Are-some-ethnic-groups-more-vulnerable-to-COVID-19-than-others-V2-IFS-Briefing-Note.pdf.

Pocock, L. (2020). 'Care Homes Have Long Been Neglected – The Pandemic Has Shown Us How Bad Things Are'. *The Conversation*. Published 8 July. Accessed 13 December 2022. https://theconversation.com/care-homes-have-long-been-neglected-the-pandemic-has-shown-us-how-bad-things-are-137458.

Porterfield, Carlie (2022). 'Companies that Rushed to Make Hand Sanitizer for Pandemic Will Now Have to Conform to FDA Guidelines'. *Forbes*. Published 21 April. Accessed 4 January 2023. https://www.forbes.com/sites/carlieporterfield/2021/10/12/companies-that-rushed-to-make-hand-sanitizer-for-pandemic-will-now-have-to-conform-to-fda-guidelines/?sh=ad726363d990.

Rage Against the Machine [@RATM] (2020). 'Washing in the name of … On this occasion it's best you do what they tell ya'. *Twitter*. Uploaded 9 March. Accessed 10 August 2020. https://twitter.com/RATM/status/1237036386886303744.

'Resilience'. *Oxford English Dictionary*. Uploaded March 2010. Accessed 15 October 2021. https://www.oed.com/view/Entry/163619?redirectedFrom=resilience#eid.

Reuters (2020). 'Johnson – Coronavirus Will Not Stop Me Shaking Hands'. Reuters. Uploaded 3 March. Accessed 3 December 2021. https://www.reuters.com/article/uk-health-coronavirus-britain-handshake-idUKKBN20Q1K2.

Ridout, N. (2009). *Theatre & Ethics*. Basingstoke: Palgrave Macmillan.

Robinson, M. (2010). 'Making Adaptive Resilience Real'. *Arts Council England*. Uploaded July. Accessed 30 December 2021. https://www.culturehive.co.uk/wp-content/uploads/2020/10/Making-adaptive-resilience-real-1.pdf.

Rogerson, E. (2020). 'The Lowry's Temporary Nightingale Courtroom: A Response'. *ayoungertheatre.com*. 26 September. Accessed 9 September 2022. https://www.ayoungertheatre.com/the-lowrys-temporary-nightingale-courtroom-a-response/.

Rosen, M. (2021). 'We're Paying the Price of the UK Government's Herd Immunity Policy'. *The Guardian*. Uploaded 20 August. Accessed 3 December 2021. https://www.theguardian.com/world/2021/aug/20/were-paying-the-price-of-the-uk-governments-herd-immunity-policy.

Runswick-Cole, K., and Goodley, D. (2013). 'Resilience: A Disability Studies and Community Psychology Approach'. *Social and Personality Psychology Compass*, 7.2: 67–78.

Rutter, M. (1987). 'Psychosocial Resilience and Protective Mechanisms'. *American Journal of Orthopsychiatry*, 57: 316–331.

Ryan. [@RyanA____] (2021). 'F*cking hell they have done a drone display of Captain Tom Moore. This country is ridiculous'. *Twitter*. Uploaded 1 January. Accessed 24 February 2021. https://twitter.com/RyanA____/status/1344796542134333442.

Saito, M. (2021). 'Japan's Tsunami Survivors Call Lost Loves on the Phone of the Wind'. *Reuters* website. Uploaded 5 March. Accessed 12 October 2022. https://www.reuters.com/article/us-japan-fukushima-anniversary-telephone-idUSKCN2AX03J.

Sample, I. (2021). 'BMA to Issue Damning Critique of Government over Covid Crisis'. *The Guardian*. Uploaded 13 September. Accessed 8 November 2021. https://www.theguardian.com/world/2021/sep/13/bma-issue-damning-critique-uk-government-covid-crisis-pandemic-nhs.

Saville, A. (2020). 'Theatre's Left Behind Freelancers. *Exeunt*. Uploaded 10 May . Accessed 28 December 2021. http://exeuntmagazine.com/features/theatres-left-behind-freelancers/.

Selman, L. E., Sowden, R. and Borgstrom, E. (2021). '"Saying Goodbye" during the COVID-19 Pandemic: A Document Analysis of Online Newspapers with Implications for End of Life Care'. *Palliative Medicine*, 35.7, July: 1277–87.

Sense8 [Television drama]. (2015). Dir. The Wachowskis. USA: Netflix.

Serafino, M., Monteiro, H. S., Shaojun, L., Reis, Saulo D. S., Igual, C., Neto, A. S. L, Travizano, M., Andrade, Jr., H. S. and Makse, H. A. (2022). 'Digital Contact Tracing and Network Theory to Stop the Spread of COVID-19 Using Big-Data on Human Mobility Geolocalization'. *PLOS Computational Biology*. Published 11 April. Accessed 10 January 2023. https://doi.org/10.1371/journal.pcbi.1009865.

Shahbaz, A., and Funk, A. (2021). 'Freedom on the Net 2021: The Global Drive to Control Big Tech'. *Freedom House*. Accessed 23 December. https://freedomhouse.org/sites/default/files/2021-09/FOTN_2021_Complete_Booklet_09162021_FINAL_UPDATED.pdf.

Sharkey, N. (2012). 'Killing Made Easy: From Joysticks to Politics'. In *Robot Ethics: The Ethical and Social Implications of Robotics*, ed. Patrick Lin, Keith Abney and George Bekey, 122. Cambridge: MIT Press.

Siddique, H., and Marsh, S. (2020). 'Coronavirus: Britons Saying Final Goodbyes to Dying Relatives by Videolink'. *The Guardian*. Uploaded 24 March. Accessed 4 December 2021. https://www.theguardian.com/world/2020/mar/24/britons-saying-final-goodbyes-to-dying-relatives-by-videolink-covid-19.

Skeete-Cross, J. (2020). 'How to Dress from the Waist Up for Your Zoom Meetings', *Evening Standard*. Uploaded 23 March. Accessed 17 October 2021. https://www.standard.co.uk/lifestyle/esmagazine/work-from-home-fashion-video-calling-waist-up-outfits-a4395406.html.

Skymagic. (2020). 'London New Year's Eve'. Accessed 2 November 2021. https://skymagic.show/project/london-new-years-eve/.

Skypower Aerial Filming (2021). 'Bloomsbury Lanes Bowling – Cinewhoop FPV'. *Vimeo*. Uploaded 29 March. Accessed 20 December 2021. https://vimeo.com/530547247#_=_.

Snow, O. (2022). 'Magic Avatar' App Lensa Generated Nudes from My Childhood Photos'. *Wired*. Published 7 December. Accessed 4 January 2023. https://www.wired.com/story/lensa-artificial-intelligence-csem/.

Stecklow, S. (2018). 'Hatebook: A Reuters Special Report'. *Reuters*. Uploaded 15 August. Accessed 7 October 2021. https://www.reuters.com/investigates/special-report/myanmar-facebook-hate/.

Steffen, L. (2020). 'Police in Spain Are Using Drones to Scold People Breaking Quarantine'. *Intelligent Living*. Published 31 March. Accessed 13 December 2022. https://www.intelligentliving.co/police-spain-drones-scold-people-breaking-quarantine/.

Stewart-Fisher, A., and Thompson, J. (2020). *Performing Care: New Perspectives on Socially Engaged Performance*. Manchester: Manchester University Press.

Suleiman, F., and Ferguson, A. (2022). 'What a Tragic Day': British Nurses Strike in Bitter Pay Dispute'. *Reuters*. Published 15 December. Accessed 7 January 2023. https://www.reuters.com/world/uk/british-nurses-begin-first-ever-strike-pay-dispute-deepens-2022-12-15/.

Svich, C. [@Csvich] (2021). 'Theatre, we're interpandemic. This is accelerated climate change. 2019 is not coming back. There isn't a reset. The mode forward is hybrid. Embrace audio, digital, streaming, & hybrid. Together we can imagine a more accessible, inventive, equitable field. While we're still here'. *Twitter*. Uploaded 19 December. Accessed 23 December 2021. https://twitter.com/Csvich/status/1472420057703534595.

'Synk' (2021). *Aespa Wiki*. Published 23 October. Accessed 13 January 2023. https://aespa.fandom.com/wiki/SYNK.

Talawa (2020a). @TalawaTheatreCo, on *Twitter*. Published 22 December. Accessed 9 September 2022. https://twitter.com/talawatheatreco/status/1341428554219859968.

Talawa (2020b). 'Talawa Issues Statement in Response to Birmingham Rep Hosting a Nightingale Court'. Accessed 2 January 2023. https://www.chloenelkinconsulting.com/news/talawa-issues-statement-in-response-to-birmingham-rep-hosting-a-nightingale-court/.

Taylor, L. (2021). 'Don't Clap for Us – We Are Not 'Heroes' – We Just Need Fair Pay, Safe Staffing and PPE, Say Nurses'. *Nursing Notes*. Uploaded 8 January . Accessed 16 November 2021. https://nursingnotes.co.uk/news/dont-clap-for-us-we-are-not-heroes-we-just-need-fair-pay-safe-staffing-and-ppe-say-nurses/#.YY6Kgi-l1p8.

Telephone (2020). [Zoom Performance] By Coney. (Perf. by Tassos Stevens). Experienced 15 October 2020.

Thomas, C. (2020). 'Resilient Health and Care: Learning the Lessons of COVID-19 in the English NHS'. Institute for Public Policy Research. Uploaded July . Accessed 10 November 2021. https://www.ippr.org/files/2020-07/resilient-health-and-care-july20.pdf.

Thompson, J. (2020). 'Towards an Aesthetics of Care'. In *Performing Care: New Perspectives on Socially Engaged Performance*, ed. Amanda Stewart Fisher and James Thompson, 36–48. Manchester: Manchester University Press.

'To Lose Face'. *Oxford English Dictionary*. Accessed 22 October 2021. https://www.oed.com/view/Entry/67425?rskey=3852PI&result=1&isAdvanced=false#eid135476900.

Trent, J. S., and Friedenberg, R. V. (2000). *Political Campaign Communication: Principles and Practices*, Fourth Edition. Westport, CT: Praeger.

Tronto, Joan C. (2013). *Caring Democracy: Markets, Equality, and Justice*. New York: New York University Press.

Tuckett, J. (2021). 'Women in Theatre Survey'. *Sphinx Theatre*. Accessed 27 December 2021. https://sphinxtheatre.co.uk/wp-content/uploads/2021/10/Women-in-Theatre-Survey-2021..pdf.

Ungar, M. (2004). 'Constructionist Discourse on Resilience: Multiple Contexts, Multiple Realities among At-Risk Children and Youth', *Youth & Society*, 35: 341–65.

Ungar, M. (2005). 'Introduction: Resilience across Cultures and Contexts'. In *Handbook for Working with Children and Youth: Pathways to Resilience Across Cultures and Contexts*, ed. M. Ungar, xv–xxxix. Thousand Oaks, CA: Sage.

UNICEF (2021). 'No-One Is Safe until Everyone Is Safe – Why We Need a Global Response to COVID-19'. Uploaded 24 May. Accessed 31 December 2021. https://www.unicef.org/press-releases/no-one-safe-until-everyone-safe-why-we-need-global-response-covid-19.

Valerian and the City of a Thousand Planets (2017). [Film] Dir. Luc Besson.

Wade, Laura (2021). 'Lack of Support for Theatre Is to Discourage Dissent, Says Top Playwright'. *The Guardian*. Uploaded 25 June. Accessed 22 October 2021. https://www.theguardian.com/stage/2021/jun/25/laura-wade-theatre-posh-home-im-darling-government-cuts-arts.

Walker, B., and Salt, D. (2006). *Resilience Thinking: Sustaining Ecosystems and People in Changing World*. Washington: Island Press.

Wang, L., Zhang Y., Wang, D., Tong, X., Liu, T., Zhang, S., Huang, J., Zhang, L., Chen, L., Fan, H. and Clarke, M. (2021). 'Artificial Intelligence for COVID-19: A Systematic Review'. *Frontiers in Medicine*, 8: 704256.

Ward, James J. (2020). 'Why the Dancing Robots Are a Really, Really Big Problem'. *Medium*. Uploaded 30 December. Accessed 8 November 2021. https://medium.com/swlh/why-the-dancing-robots-are-a-really-really-big-problem-4faa22c7f899.

Weisbrode, K., and Yeung, H. H. (2020). 'Resilience Theatre'. *Royal United Services Institute (RUSI)* website. Published 29 April. Accessed 14 October 2022. https://rusi.org/explore-our-research/publications/commentary/resilience-theatre.

Welz, C. (2011). 'Shame and the Hiding Self', *Passions in Context: International Journal for the History and Theory of Emotions*, Atrocities – Emotion – Self, 2: 67–92.

White, C. (2020). 'We Must See through the Veil of Veneration Surrounding Captain Tom Moore'. *Varsity*. Uploaded 1 May. Accessed 8 November 2021. https://www.varsity.co.uk/opinion/19121.

Williams, S. N., and Dienes, K. (2020). 'Coronavirus: New Social Rules Are Leading to New Types of Stigma'. *The Conservation*. Uploaded 22 July. Accessed 30 November 2022. https://theconversation.com/coronavirus-new-social-rules-are-leading-to-new-types-of-stigma-142885.

Williamson, G. (2021). 'Notification to the Office for Students (OfS) by the Secretary of State for Education to Set Terms and Conditions for the Allocation by OfS of Strategic Priorities Grant Funding for the 2021/22 Academic Year'. *Office for Students*. Uploaded 19 July. Accessed 22 October. https://www.officeforstudents.org.uk/media/0e833c6f-c355-4743-8953-071bbe9b1518/ts-and-cs-on-recurrent-funding-19-july.pdf.

Wood, H., and Skeggs, B. (2020). 'Clap for Carers? From Care Gratitude to Care Justice'. *European Journal of Cultural Studies*, 23.4: 641–7.

World Health Organisation (2020). 'COVID-19 – China'. *World Health Organisation* website. Uploaded 5 January. Accessed 13 November 2022. https://www.who.int/emergencies/disease-outbreak-news/item/2020-DON229.

Worthen, W. B. (2021). 'Zoom; or, Obsolescence'. *TDR: The Drama Review*, 65.3: 181–200.

Young, A., Green, L. and Rogers, K. D. (2008). 'Resilience and Deaf Children: A Literature Review'. *Deafness Education International*, 10: 40–55.

Žižek, S. (1999). 'Is It Possible to Traverse the Fantasy in Cyberspace?' In *The Žižek Reader*, ed. Elizabeth Wright and Edmond Wright, 102–24. Malden, MA: Blackwell Publishing.

Žižek, S. (2004). 'A Plea for Ethical Violence'. *The Bible and Critical Theory*, 1. Accessed 22 November 2022. https://citeseerx.ist.psu.edu/viewdoc/download?doi=10.1.1.970.7854&rep=rep1&type=pdf.

Zuckerberg, M. (2021). 'Facebook Connect 2021'. *Facebook*. Published 28 October. Accessed 4 January 2023. https://www.facebook.com/Meta/videos/facebook-connect-2021/577658430179350/.

INDEX

Index

Index

www.ingramcontent.com/pod-product-compliance
Lightning Source LLC
LaVergne TN
LVHW010927110826
845149LV00013B/2513

* 9 7 8 1 3 5 0 2 7 2 1 1 8 *